# PRAISE FOR *SPEAK UP* AND LINDA MASON

"At a time when TV news has been demonized and polarized, it's refreshing to read this colorful memoir by a groundbreaking journalist whose intelligence, integrity, and good humor propelled her to great heights—through the glass ceiling and beyond." —**Andrew Heyward**, former president, CBS News

"Linda Mason blazed a trail across the tough and sometimes hostile terrain of network TV news and helped clear a path for every woman who followed her. It's an inspiring story of brains, guts, and determination along with a colorful insider's account of one of America's most celebrated institutions by a pioneer who was there every step of the way—whether the guys liked it or not." —**Marcy McGinnis**, former Sr. Vice President, CBS News

"Linda Mason shows us what it took to report pivotal moments in history. At a time when trust in the news media needs it most, Linda explains the extraordinary work it took to get the story right, and the importance given to that effort. While she downplays just how remarkable it was that she, a woman, had a seat at the table, Linda Mason was at the center of that critical moment in the life of some of the most important stories of our time." —**Elisa Lees Muñoz**, executive director, International Women's Media Foundation

"Women everywhere are in debt to Linda Mason. Her perseverance helped make CBS News vibrant with the contributions of women and people of color. *Speak Up* is a fight for justice wrapped in the amazing adventures of an intrepid journalist." —**Scott Pelley**, correspondent and anchor, CBS News

"Linda Mason made such a strong impression on me when I was a new Broadcast Associate through standards seminars that she ran. I still invoke her name and think of her as a holy grail of sorts for thorough, serious vetting and consideration in news reporting." —**Josh Ravitz**, senior director of rights and clearances, CBS News

"Linda Mason has been a guiding light for CBS News and the hundreds of journalists she has helped along the way. Her life served as the perfect foundation for her inspirational and pivotal role. Linda not only broke through multiple glass ceilings, but she also made sure she would help others do the same. *Speak Up* is a testament to her legacy." —**Alturo Rhymes**, executive story editor, *CBS Evening News*

"I don't think there's another woman who could write a memoir like Linda Mason's. She was usually the only 'she' in the room, influencing and shaping news coverage at CBS News for 30 years of major historical events. She writes colorfully about collaborating with Walter Cronkite and Dan Rather, about navigating and handling the #MeToo moments, and about juggling a big job with kids and a husband. She was in the room with real power. It's an extraordinary news flash and a wonderful book." —**Lesley Stahl**, journalist, CBS News and *60 Minutes*

"Among the women pioneers in broadcast news, Linda Mason is best positioned to share invaluable context and perspective in her rise through the predicaments of gender politics at CBS where her talent and persistence prevailed." —**Matthew Winkler**, co-founder and editor-in-chief emeritus, Bloomberg News

# SPEAK UP

## Breaking the Glass Ceiling at *CBS News*

LINDA MASON

Foreword by Connie Chung

ROWMAN & LITTLEFIELD
*Lanham • Boulder • New York • London*

Published by Rowman & Littlefield
An imprint of The Rowman & Littlefield Publishing Group, Inc.
4501 Forbes Boulevard, Suite 200, Lanham, Maryland 20706
www.rowman.com

86-90 Paul Street, London EC2A 4NE

British Library Cataloguing in Publication Information Available

**Library of Congress Cataloging-in-Publication Data**

Names: Mason, Linda, author. | Chung, Connie, writer of foreword.
Title: Speak up : breaking the glass ceiling at CBS News / Linda Mason ;
   foreword by Connie Chung.
Description: Lanham : Rowman & Littlefield, 2023. | Includes index.
Identifiers: LCCN 2022055835 (print) | LCCN 2022055836 (ebook) | ISBN
   9781538176405 (cloth) | ISBN 9781538176412 (ebook)
Subjects: LCSH: Mason, Linda. | Women television producers and
   directors—United States—Biography. | Television broadcasting of
   news—United States. | CBS News—Biography. | LCGFT: Autobiographies.
Classification: LCC PN1992.4.M377 A3 2023  (print) | LCC PN1992.4.M377
   (ebook) | DDC 070.92 [B]—dc23/eng/20230206
LC record available at https://lccn.loc.gov/2022055835
LC ebook record available at https://lccn.loc.gov/2022055836

# CONTENTS

# FOREWORD

## Connie Chung

It was the fall of 1971. The women's movement had taken hold and the male-dominated TV news world was forced to take notice. CBS News executives went on a guilt trip. Four women were hired in one fell swoop: Sylvia Chase in New York City, Michelle Clark in Chicago, and Lesley Stahl and me at the coveted Washington Bureau, where the best of the best called home. It didn't matter that Lesley and I were relegated to sit in sixth-grade school desks—the chair wrapped around us to the desk. We obediently sat in a hallway in a row, one behind the next. Never mind that we were called reporters, not correspondents. We were working at CBS Network News—our dream destination.

Every producer was a man. Every executive, a man. Every correspondent, a man other than the lone woman, Marya McLaughlin, the first woman reporter at CBS News.

But hold on!

In New York at CBS News headquarters, there was one shining beacon on whom we could rely—Linda Mason, the first woman producer for Walter Cronkite's number one news broadcast, *The CBS Evening News with Walter Cronkite*.

For me it was the beginning of a twenty-five-year relationship with this award-winning journalist, news executive, and friend, Linda Mason, who nurtured me, encouraged me, and believed so much in my succeeding.

Linda had only just been elevated to the producer ranks, hired by Sandy Socolow, the same liberated executive who supported me time and again when I was climbing the network ladder. Sandy had recognized early on how professional Linda was in having to endure those battle scars from the all-male newsroom. It didn't take Linda long before she was noticed by the higher-ups. All during the 1972 presidential campaign, she was producing many of the primary reports for Cronkite himself.

As Lesley and I began reporting on the Watergate scandal, there was Linda working on the newly formed *CBS Evening News* investigative unit that handled much of our reporting. She was always there dealing with "the boys," who weren't about to cede their turf to these two young "skirts."

Linda showed us another side of herself, which I didn't take advantage of until much later—the working mom. She did it all during an age that the issue was an unspoken, private struggle—balancing work and motherhood.

She helped produce the CBS News investigative special, puncturing the music industry, targeting the company's own CBS Records, one of the largest music producers in the world, outlining the "pay for play" scandal. It was payola in the form of gifts and drugs to radio disc jockeys by the music companies (including CBS Records, one of the largest moneymakers in the CBS family).

Later, CBS executives realized what a hard-nosed, honest producer Linda was when she and CBS News were sued by one of the witnesses who claimed his remarks were wrongly edited. Linda showed the judge how that was false. The judge ended the trial in favor of Linda and CBS News.

I left the Washington Bureau of CBS News in 1976 to anchor local news at the CBS-owned and -operated station in Los Angeles, so I wasn't there for the rocket ride Linda was on as she continued to break glass. No woman had the responsibilities she had from the 1980s on. She was the executive producer for both the Saturday editions and Sunday editions of the *CBS Weekend News*, plus Charles Kuralt's *CBS Sunday Morning*, the broadcast that brought smiles to so many millions each week.

When I rejoined CBS News in 1989 after my Los Angeles assignment and six years at NBC News, I felt as if I was returning home. We were reunited on the *CBS Sunday News*—she, as the executive producer and I, as anchor. As I watched Linda juggle those three programs with a typical skeleton weekend staff, I remember thinking, *How does she do it? How does she produce multiple programs with no muss, no fuss, no frenzy? Always calm.*

And then there were all the seminal events she covered, the trips to Moscow, Vietnam, and China.

What joy I had when, in 1992, Linda Mason became a real-life heavyweight in the news division, a full-fledged vice president. Linda was at the helm when I started a magazine program, *Eye to Eye with Connie Chung*. She became the executive in charge of the prime-time weekly program. From then onward, Linda was given responsibilities only a grown-up could handle—troublesome, serious issues that needed to be led by someone who had credibility and integrity. She headed the internal investigation into the calling of the 2000 election that CBS News as well as other news organizations botched. The conclusions she reached and the standards put in place hold up today on election night more than twenty years later.

And then there was the scandal surrounding the *60 Minutes* report from producer Mary Mapes and Dan Rather, the longtime anchor of the network's flagship broadcast, the *CBS Evening News*. The report aired in 2004—an investigation into President George W. Bush's service in the National Guard. The president of the CBS corporation, Les Moonves, and CBS News president Andrew Hayward entrusted Linda to be the liaison to the outside panel investigating the story. The findings led to the firing of Mapes and Rather's exit from the anchor desk.

I have known the handful of women executives in the television news business who followed in Linda Mason's footsteps. It was by no means an easy road to navigate. The respect Linda earned may have been grudging at first, but even the crusty old goats we all tolerated came around in the end to take her seriously, as well they should have. She was truly worthy of the status she achieved. As you turn each page of her book, you will see why.

# INTRODUCTION

CBS correspondent and anchor Charles Kuralt once said of me, "[Linda] is a mountain climber. I think she feels at home at the top. She knows how to report and write; she can lead, follow, or get the hell out of the way." Thinking about this observation, I realized that Kuralt had summed me up in a few, well-chosen phrases.

I would like to share with you how for more than fifty years as a woman journalist I blazed a trail working at two city newspapers, one while in high school and the other while in college, then at CBS News from one of the lowest positions, desk assistant in radio, to one of the highest, senior vice president.

Much of what I am going to share I learned in retrospect, looking back on my career to write this memoir. The lessons are valid today. I hope that you, the reader, can incorporate some of them as you proceed toward your goals in journalism or any other career.

When I became a journalist, newspapers and radio were the dominant information delivery systems. Television news was in its infancy and would not come of age until the mid-1960s, just as I was beginning my career. And now in the twenty-first century, news has gone digital. Hands that once held ink-smeared broadsheets and tabloids with day-old news now clasp sleek and shiny cell phones that can provide news as it happens, with live pictures and sound. Newspapers are struggling to survive, morphing into online journalism. As the transition occurs, more than two thousand print newspapers have folded, putting tens of thousands of journalists out of work.

When I began at CBS News, network news was considered a public service. The networks funded news with the huge profits from their sports and entertainment divisions. Today, network news is required to pay for itself and make its own profits. Since the mid-1980s this has led to major downsizing and layoffs in news departments. But there is hope as more and more journalists and news organizations create new ways to finance their reporting. Some are turning to contributions and grants from the public in a kind of 501(c) nonprofit system.

What we see on our TV screen when we tune in for news is changing as well. The programs are often more opinion than objective reporting, and viewers tend to choose the stations and commentators with whom they agree. Journalists had always declared they covered events from all angles, but that basic precept seems to be ignored today.

As I began my journalism career in the early 1960s, there was little discrimination against women because there were very few women in the profession. I didn't realize until I started climbing the ladder that this was a men's club. Reality was a shock—when, having done producer work for several years, I was told "women could not be producers." I fought back, finally smashing the glass ceiling at CBS News.

I pursued my career with blinders on. I kept my eye on the prize—the next job, and rarely thought, I can't reach that because I am a woman. Also, in retrospect, I was shielded from negative male comments. At my second job, at CBS Radio, I worked as a researcher for the radio correspondent Allan Jackson, and months later I became a writer, with two other writers, both male, at CBS News Syndication. These were small shops and the men were my supporters, not hecklers.

In the following pages, I will share the story of my half century as a journalist, fortunate enough to lead some of the next generation of female journalists through the crack in the glass at CBS News while covering important news events of the last quarter of the twentieth century. What I learned along the way I now share with young women and men as they begin their chosen professions. The tips are simple: Work hard, ask questions, and when the time is right, *Speak Up*.

Working hard needs no explanation. I completed every job even if it took until after my shift ended. As you'll see my shifts were not always at the best times: in my first job I worked 5:00 a.m. to 1:00 p.m. and had Tuesdays and Wednesdays off. In later jobs I worked weekends as well, but during the day!

When you are asked to do something you don't understand: *ask*. No one will think badly of you. But if through a misunderstanding you deliver the wrong product, you will be judged.

And finally, having built a record of good work, *speak up* and ask your boss what the next step is. Ask for help getting there.

My career began when in January 1966, after five months of unemployment and a few freelance assignments in New York City, I was offered a job as a desk assistant at CBS Radio. Although it was one of the lowest rungs on the ladder, equivalent to a copyboy at a newspaper, I was ecstatic. I worked from 5:00 a.m. to 1:00 p.m. and learned about CBS News.

Within several months, I was promoted to researcher (same hours) and after four months promoted again to news writer at CBS News Syndication. In analyzing these promotions, I realized I had worked very hard each day and asked questions when I was unsure where to go. I made friends along the way who helped me on my path. For instance, when a friend was leaving his writing job, he suggested I apply. I did, got the job, and learned to write television reports over a two-year period, tutored by my fellow writers. I always had my eye on the ball, perfecting my skills. I continued to meet people at CBS and another contact told me about an opening at the morning news shop. I applied and got the job. In retrospect, I see how important this constant networking was in increasing my contacts, which helped me move on in my quest to become a producer. This was not planned. But I now realize that working hard to perfect my job abilities and meeting people at work were two important aspects of my progress and could be important examples for you to follow.

I also want to share some of my reporting adventures with you. I took Dan Rather to interview Fidel Castro and tour Cuba. There were some surprises along the way. Castro was friendly and apparently open to us, and we were able to ask about the repression in his country.

In Vietnam we were surprised that both our former ally (the South Vietnamese) and our former enemy (the North Vietnamese) were friendly and welcoming. People in Hanoi, the Northern victors in the Vietnam War, felt superior to the South Vietnamese, although the South was modernizing at a much more rapid pace than the North. There was also drama in Vietnam as General Norman Schwarzkopf relived his tours of duty there.

When we went to Washington to testify at the hearings on the election error of 2000, we got a close-up, nitty-gritty show of the congressional and federal political system.

Our reporting on the CBS Bagdad tragedy brought us to Landstuhl, Germany, where Correspondent Kimberly Dozier was airlifted to recover from the life-threatening wounds she sustained in a Baghdad attack. Landstuhl cares for soldiers wounded abroad, such as in Iraq, Afghanistan, and other hotspots where Americans are stationed. It was the most modern medical facility I had ever seen. It was ready twenty-four hours a day to accept the most severely wounded.

There were other adventures and several sobering incidents, such as a mistake CBS News made that almost destroyed the network's credibility. Through it all, I learned the basic tenets of journalism and how to lead when a crisis develops.

I think your takeaway from this book should be three phrases: 1. Work hard 2. Ask questions 3. *Speak Up!* Oh, and don't forget to be patient!

# 1

# HELLO, FIDEL!

I tossed and turned in bed on that June night in 1996. One agonizing question was keeping me awake: Will he, or won't he? "He" was Fidel Castro, the flamboyant leader of the Cuban revolution and president of the island nation since 1959. I wondered will he or won't he give us an interview? In just a few hours, I would be flying to Cuba with CBS News correspondent and anchor Dan Rather, two producers, and two video crews. I had met Castro the previous fall when he visited CBS News headquarters in New York. He was in town for the fiftieth anniversary of the United Nations. I was sure Castro would not remember me, but I could not forget his magnetic personality.

Although the United States and Cuba are separated by ninety short miles, there is a long history of animosity. A US embargo that banned direct flights to Cuba was then in effect, so we flew from Miami to the Bahamas and then chartered a plane to the Sierra Maestra, a mountain range in southeasternmost Cuba. That is where Castro and his ragtag army began their revolution nearly forty-five years earlier and where he had agreed to talk to us. But Castro was famous for reneging on his promises to reporters, which explained my sleeplessness. There was a lot on the line and on my shoulders. I was responsible for Dan Rather, the production crew, and the charter. What if something went wrong? Would I be blamed because I was a woman?

I mentioned my worry to Dan, a Texan who offered a Las Vegas perspective. "If I were a betting man," he said, "I'd say we'll get the interview, but it may take some time, Linda. Castro is known to keep reporters waiting." Obviously, nothing was for sure. In fact, we had already hit a snag. Two days before we left New York, Castro's office informed us he would not be going to the Sierra Maestra after all. I was

1

determined to stick with the original plan. I told Rather and the crew, "Cameras are rarely allowed here, so let's get some video of the region. We can always interview Castro in Havana." Rather agreed. We landed at a small Cuban airstrip and then took a boat to the mountains, which rose dramatically from the sea. We stepped onto a very rickety dock and began our steep ascent to rebel headquarters.

I was shocked when I looked up. Like a mirage, Castro and a small entourage were walking down the steep path to greet us. Obviously there had been another change of plans. What a relief! Rather had met Castro several times, so they renewed their acquaintance with warm greetings. "Welcome to the beginning of the revolution," Castro said. "Buenos Dias," Rather replied, and introduced me to Castro. As I shook the old revolutionary's hand, I realized he was taller than I remembered and thin, and his piercing dark eyes, magnetic. He wore heavy green army fatigues and a brimmed hat, looking cool despite the eighty-degree heat.

It was immediately clear that Castro was in charge. We talked with the help of his superb interpreter, Nina, who managed to provide simultaneous translations, as if Castro, Rather, and I were speaking to each other directly. Castro turned to me and asked, "Where would you like to begin?" I replied, "From the beginning." By that, I meant the revolution itself. I was certain I sounded calm, but in any case, I was incredulous. Here, standing next to me, was the world-famous Fidel Castro, in the flesh, pleased to see Rather and me, offering to lead us on our mission to see his country.

Castro invited us to walk the steep trail that led to a clearing that had been the "Holy Land" of the Cuban revolution: lush green mountains with peaks so tall, the clouds seemed to get stuck between their spires. It was quiet and hot. I visualized the rebels these mountains had supported during the revolution: the downtrodden farmers and city workers fed up with their lives of poverty, willing to depose Fulgencio Batista, Cuba's US-backed dictator. Castro told Rather that he had been "happier here than anywhere else because everything—the revolution and its aftermath—were still ahead." Rather later told me, "Castro had what I would describe as a thousand-year stare, looking way in the distance." He asked Castro, "What are you thinking?" Castro replied, "I wish time would stand still."

As we toured portions of the old base, Castro, a great storyteller, was delighted to share some of his favorites. It was a pleasure to be in his company, hearing firsthand the details of his many adventures. "This was home to the revolutionaries who fled Mexico with me and the fighters who joined us." He related the horror of crossing back to Cuba from Mexico in November of 1956 aboard the yacht *Granma*, built to accommodate twelve but now carrying nearly seven times that number. "Of the eighty-two revolutionaries crammed on the *Granma*, only nineteen made it back to this camp," Castro said as he winced. "The rest died of sickness or at the hands of Cuban soldiers." But starting with fewer than two dozen men, Castro waged a successful revolution, one of the most significant in Cold War history.

Other stories followed: "Here is where the first muskets were hidden," he said, pointing to a field. "We had a shooting range for practice over there in the dense vegetation. In the beginning, our headquarters moved a lot. We knew all the paths, and in the dark of the night, I could find my way around." Nina relayed each of his comments. After several hours at the old camp, we were guided to our helicopter, Castro to his. Helicopters were the only way to cover long distances in Cuba since the roads had deteriorated badly, and it was nearly five hundred miles to Havana. We flew over tobacco fields that extended as far as the eye could see, raw material for the world-famous Cuban cigars. Miles of sugarcane spread out below, long used in Cuba and the rest of the Caribbean to make rum. Castro told us later, "The revolution was partly to empower the farmers."

Finally, we reached Havana. Our formal interview with the president was set for late the next evening. Dan and I thought it would be our final visit with Castro, but he was full of surprises and we could not have been more wrong. Unannounced, he appeared at many other sites, ultimately joining us for more than half our three-day visit and serving as an invigorating guide.

"Havana has changed dramatically," I told Rather, something I knew firsthand. My family vacationed in Cuba several times in the late 1950s when it bustled as the most cosmopolitan city in the Caribbean. It was glamorous. The wealthy from around the world spent big money in the casinos. Gambling, tourism, and, of course, cigars and rum fueled Cuba's economy.

"Looking at Havana today, I wouldn't have imagined that," Rather replied. "Paint is peeling off most of the buildings and the fancy tiled sidewalks are in ruins. People are so plainly dressed." Indeed, the glamour and vivacity of the Havana I had known as a teenager was long gone.

The next day we flew about a hundred miles to the Bay of Pigs, site of one of the ugliest chapters in US–Cuban history. It was a beautiful day, and the bay was gorgeous: aquamarine water gently lapped the white sandy beaches. Rather had waded into the bay to record a portion of our documentary when we suddenly heard the whir of helicopter blades. Sure enough, Fidel Castro had dropped in, again, to personally show us the place where, in 1961, the US government had coordinated a military maneuver in its first attempt to overthrow the new communist government of the Republic of Cuba. An American force of CIA-trained Cuban exiles landed at the Bay of Pigs and almost immediately surrendered to Castro's defending troops; the promised US air support never materialized. Castro held the shocked and disappointed would-be "liberators" as prisoners for a solid year. The CIA called the operation, "a perfect failure."

Over the years, there would be hundreds of attempts on Castro's life. All of them failed, leading Castro to say, "If surviving assassination attempts were an Olympic event, I would win a gold medal."

With the United States as his enemy, Castro reached out to the Soviet Union for military support. The Soviet leader, Nikita Khrushchev, was quick to take advantage of an alliance with a country so close to the US mainland. He taunted the American government in October of 1962 by shipping Russian-made atomic missiles to Cuba, an event that led to the "Cuban Missile Crisis." The world held its breath as President John F. Kennedy and Premier Nikita Khrushchev negotiated a settlement, preventing all-out nuclear war. As the Soviets removed the missiles from Cuba, the world heaved a collective sigh of relief. I remember the moment well. In college at the time, I called my dad to see if he thought there could be war. "Hopefully not, but there is no guarantee," he said. This incident led people to label Castro a communist. Castro told us he was never a communist, but rather "a socialist seeking to make a better life for Cuba."

Castro was eager to show us the Museo Giron, the Bay of Pigs Museum. We saw, up-close, artifacts of the failed American invasion.

For us, it was embarrassing and awkward, as Castro enjoyed pointing out items recovered from the invaders: lighters, guns, and parts of American uniforms, such as belts and boots.

While Rather and Castro were engaged in animated conversation with Nina's help, one of the security people approached me. "Senora," he said, "the helicopter that carried Senor Rather has a broken engine." My heart sank. What to do? I had an idea. "Can you get a bus to take Rather and our crew to Havana?" I knew Cuba no longer had relations with the Soviet Union, for years its supplier of spare parts. But the resourcefulness of Cuban mechanics was legendary. They could keep engines running using scraps of metal and parts from old generators and lawn mowers. One of the memorable sights of our trip was the American cars from the 1950s, literally held together by chicken wire, crowding Havana's busy boulevards. Still, when the security officer returned to say, "Senora, the helicopter has been fixed, you can fly back," I was plenty anxious. Do I endanger the anchor of the *CBS Evening News* or play it safe and go by bus? Rather's decision, "Let's fly." And off we went.

Our trip back to Havana became a tribute to the revolution. We landed several times, once to visit an elementary school and a second to visit a hospital. "Education and the medical system are twin pillars of the revolution," Castro proclaimed. It was estimated that nearly 100 percent of the population was literate, and medical care was free.

On the ground at the school, students and townspeople gathered in a big crowd shouting, "Fidel! Fidel! Fidel," and singing the national anthem. When we landed again, this time at a hospital, there was a repeat performance as the medical staff raced out to cheer, "Fidel! Fidel! Fidel." It was exciting and unreal as if we were in a movie. Castro's energy was infectious.

We finally landed in Havana and went off to prepare for our interview with Castro at nine o'clock that night.

The president appeared for the interview dressed in a dark suit, white shirt, and tie, looking like a movie star playing Castro. He was eager to share his thoughts about the revolution and his early life. The interview lasted three hours, ending at midnight. "I lived alongside the laborers on my father's finca," he said. The finca, or farm, was a twenty-five-thousand-acre sugar plantation with four hundred and forty workers. "I was born Catholic, baptized but left the Church during the Revolution." He also declared, "I still have Catholic roots and have invited the Pope to visit." John Paul II did visit Cuba in January of 1998, a year and a half after our visit.

Rather asked Castro many questions about why he had seen the need for revolution. In reply, Castro described what had been and what he was still trying to accomplish. "We are seeking a system that will give people dignity. People are tired and fed up with corruption, racial and sexual discrimination." And he emphasized, "This is a socialist revolution, *not* a Communist one."

Rather and I were impressed by Castro's fervor and idealism. He seemed honest and moral, truly taken by the interests of his people and his country's well-being. But we also knew that tens of thousands of Cubans who opposed Castro had fled to the United States, many risking their lives in the 1980 Mariel boatlift, others in lesser-known journeys by sea. Whatever their status, all were fleeing what they considered a dictatorship and stringent economic measures. Even one of Castro's sisters, Juanita Castro, fled to Miami, saying that while she supported the revolution in the beginning, "I could no longer support Fidel's methods of repression."

For instance, Castro declared it unlawful to challenge him. Anyone who disobeyed could end up in jail or dead. When asked about this, Castro said firmly, "The counter-revolutionaries do not have the prerogative of the revolutionaries to dissent." He gave no more details than this, no more reasons. I found his dictatorial mantra frightening, underlying his worst destructive measures.

As the interview continued, Castro started to sweat under the hot lights. One of the CBS cameramen tentatively asked me, "Would you powder his face with a powder puff to dry it?" That's what is done in a hot television studio to dry the sweat. I said, "No, it doesn't feel right." But then he suggested I use a certain kind of paper embedded with powder. I said "Fine," so I went to Castro and asked, "May I please pat this on your face?" He smiled. I then whispered to Rather, "I need to pat this paper on your face or Castro might get suspicious." He nodded, smiling as well.

It was midnight when we finished and then went to a different floor in the building for a very late dinner. I was amazed to be seated next to Castro. His place card read "El Jefe," the boss, one of Castro's nicknames. I was seized with the fantasy of grabbing that place card at the end of the meal, as a souvenir, but I restrained myself. As dinner began, Castro, through Nina, told me, "This first course of crayfish is my own recipe." I watched his eyes sparkle as he went on, "It was one of my contributions to meals at the camp." The course was delicious. During the meal, Castro entertained us with more stories of the revolution. At meal's end, he passed out cigars to everyone, including me. He did not take one for himself, saying, "I stopped smoking several years ago."

We saw Castro one last time as we finished an early morning shoot. He met us at the museum housing the *Granma*, the yacht that carried Castro and his revolutionaries to Cuba from their exile in Mexico. He had come to tell us again about that harrowing journey that only a handful survived.

We flew home that afternoon and began editing this historic treasure into a one-hour special, reporting the good as well as the bad. On the one hand, I was awed and appreciative of the whole experience because Castro, a man of great strength, had been warm and engaging. I enjoyed learning so much about him and the Cuban people. Yet I also knew that despite the positive experiences and colorful stories, Castro was capable of great cruelty. His dictatorial persona had punished a multitude of Cubans, many of whom, half a century after the revolution, still yearn for freedom and a better life.

*CBS Reports: Profile of a Revolutionary* gave Americans a rare look at Fidel Castro and his dictatorship, a world away from the small suburban town where my own story began.

# 2

# GROWING UP

I grew up in a small suburb of the biggest city in the United States. We were only sixty miles north of New York City, but Middletown was middle America. Drive ten minutes from this town of twenty-thousand and you were in dairy country, replete with fields of green grass and milk cows grazing against a backdrop of red barns. I have always thought of Middletown as quintessential America. Growing up there gave me easy entry to the many people I interviewed across the country. I was not from New York City, but from a town like theirs.

My journalism career began in the summer of 1959 working for the local newspaper. I had been elected editor of the high school newspaper for my senior year and I wanted to see firsthand what a professional editor does. My first assignment was as an assistant to the women's page editor, keeping calendars of events, recipes, and wedding and engagement announcements. But I was in the newsroom and was excited by the reporters and editors yelling out headlines and the wire machines typing away. This was the *news*. I took a deep breath.

When my boss went on vacation, Bill Duke, the city editor, oversaw her beat. He sent me on my first assignment, an interview with the head of the Salvation Army in Orange County to learn the amazing work these dedicated people provide. A photo I took of the woman who headed this unit appeared in the paper, right above my first-ever byline.

I wrote and re-wrote and re-wrote the story until my typewriter ribbon was practically worn out. With trepidation, I delivered the draft. Duke took my copy, put it through his typewriter, and made one edit that would change my life. He added, "by Linda Mason."

*This is it*, I thought. *I'm on my way.*

I soon found out the importance of what came after my name—the entire reputation of the news service that I represented. Growing up, I didn't have a lot of confidence and was somewhat shy. But when I could say, "I am Linda Mason, reporter for the *Middletown Record* or later, the *Providence (RI) Journal*," or better yet, "Linda Mason from CBS News," I was a different person. With the reporter's title, I felt I could go anywhere and meet anyone.

And I did. I went to Cuba to interview Fidel Castro, took General Norman Schwarzkopf back to Vietnam twenty years after the war had ended, and was in Beijing's Tiananmen Square when it was stormed by Chinese revolutionaries. I did not do this alone, of course. I had a lot of support. But there was a time when I didn't have support and when being a woman in what was then a man's profession was very difficult. During my forty-seven-year career at CBS News, I was the first woman in many of the jobs I held. I did not set out to break barriers, but when I did, it was largely the result of very hard work and of not being afraid to speak up when the opportunities presented themselves.

My dad, Dr. Harry Mason, was a huge force in my life. His parents came from Russia and settled in Asbury Park, New Jersey. He was one of two brothers who went to college while his three sisters worked. He was a dentist and oral surgeon who had wanted to be a writer, a doctor, and an actor. My brother, sister, and I fulfilled his dreams in different ways. I was the writer, my brother a vascular surgeon, my sister a ballet dancer. Dad read my work and could be a tough critic. He called many of my newspaper reports mediocre, but highly praised others.

Dad encouraged me to participate in a freedom ride in 1963. Groups across the country were protesting segregation and the curbing of civil rights—especially in the South, where buses, restrooms, and lunch counters had designated areas marked "colored only" and "Whites only." Police officers enforced the laws, arresting large numbers of Blacks and whites as they sat side by side at lunch counters and marched shoulder to shoulder in the streets.

I boarded a bus with Brown University students in Providence, Rhode Island, to participate in a freedom ride to Glen Bernie, Maryland (just south of Baltimore). We stopped for a church service and were regaled with passionate speeches about racial equality and felt a wave of spiritual fortitude as we sang "We Shall Overcome." We then went to a strip mall where groups made up of Black and white students tried to enter various businesses. I led a group into a restaurant. The maître d' glared at us as he said, "There are no tables." I angrily pointed out that the restaurant was half empty. He finally seated us at a table near the kitchen, giving us dirty menus. I will never forget the raw hatred on the faces of the diners. Outside, the state police were milling about purportedly "to keep the order." I was never the same after that experience. After all, Maryland was hardly the "Deep South." Glen Bernie, a Baltimore suburb, was barely fifty miles south of the Mason-Dixon Line!

More than fifty years later, when George Floyd was murdered on a Minneapolis street by a white police officer, memories of those demonstrations rushed over me. They had led to the landmark 1965 Civil Rights Act, the broadest civil rights legislation since the Civil War. But the civil rights momentum of the 1960s faded, replaced by the demonstrations, in the 1970s, for and against the Vietnam War. One difference today is the widespread instantaneous digital communication that has swelled the Black Lives Matter movement.

During my junior year at Brown, Dad supported my decision to spend the summer of 1963 in Poland and Russia, with the Experiment in International Living. The program placed college students with families all over the world. I chose to go to Warsaw, Poland, to live with a family since that program also offered a trip to the USSR. The Cuban Missile Crisis had occurred the year before, when the Soviet Union transported atomic weapons to Cuba, less than a hundred miles from US shores, and there was talk of nuclear war. The United States won the battle of nerves, and the Soviets took the weapons home. International relations remained tense, and their repercussions had most Americans very scared. Spending the summer in Poland and Russia at that time was a huge leap of faith. I trusted that the people there (like the people in the United States) would not let political crises poison opportunities for human connection.

I wrote articles about my experiences in Poland and Russia for the Middletown and Providence newspapers. Since I was in my junior year at Brown, I also wrote a thesis about contemporary Poland for my honors degree in international relations.

Years later, when my dad was asked to comment about my accomplishments, he didn't mince words. "A helluva story for a little gal from Middletown," he told the local newspaper.

My mom, Betty Mason, kept the family together. From her I learned to be grounded. To be patient. To be kind. She was there for me. Before I had a driver's license, Mom drove me to the interviews I did for the local paper. My mother's family had also come from Russia. Her two brothers went to college, becoming a lawyer and an engineer. Mom and her three sisters went to work to support their brothers. When I, my brother, and sister left for college, Mom earned her bachelor's degree and taught at the local high school. Essentially, she was an early "women's libber." While proud of my career, she also urged me to live life, stressing that family is very important. She was so right, and you can imagine my tremendous shock when she died suddenly while I was seven months pregnant with my first daughter. I realize now that her death led me to build a kind of box in which I stored experiences that hurt me. As a woman struggling in a man's world, that box provided some protection. I could place incidents that deeply hurt in that box and sort through them when I was ready.

My husband and two daughters were critical partners in my career. My husband had worked for CBS News, so he understood deadlines and late nights and he helped my daughters become supportive, as well. My daughters were also fans. In the late 1970s and early 1980s, when most mothers stayed home and I was working, my girls told me it felt normal. My younger daughter said, "I'm glad you did, Mom, because it's what I want to do." Today she is a working mom.

I had another weapon in my bag: I knew I could not do everything. I learned that at age eight, when my right arm and right hand were partially paralyzed by polio. I awoke one morning with my right side greatly weakened and my right hand unable to perform normally. I could no longer function as a right-handed person, so I ate with my left hand. There was a polio pandemic sweeping the country. I was lucky to avoid spending time in an iron lung and recovered during a summer at home. I found alternative ways to perform tasks. As I grew older, typing—an essential skill for a journalist—was difficult, since my fingers were no longer flexible. But I toughed it out. Kept trying. This was clearly a lesson in knowing my limitations, but it also made me aware of my capabilities and my underlying strengths.

In fall 1965, after graduation from Brown and Syracuse University, I moved to New York City. Bouncing between unemployment and a couple of freelance jobs, I knew a whole new adventure was beginning.

My career success was not instantaneous, but my determination served me well throughout my life. It was key to surviving and thriving at the most storied broadcast news organization in America.

# 3

# CBS—HERE I AM

In January of 1966, CBS was at the top of the network news business, and I was about to start my career there—at the very bottom.

It was a bleak Sunday afternoon, but a bright new world awaited me inside the CBS Broadcast Center on the West Side of Manhattan. Nervous and excited, I walked cautiously from the subway down West 57th Street as a cold wind whipped off the Hudson River. In those days, this was a rough part of town. It was 4:00 p.m. (on this winter afternoon) and already dark outside. I arrived an hour early for my shift. My heart was beating wildly, and I couldn't imagine what lay ahead.

As I entered the ground-floor lobby, the guard asked, "Your name?" He called the newsroom, and someone came to escort me. I had worked in the *Providence Journal* newsroom, which was very large, and I had also seen the even larger *New York Times* newsroom. But that day, I entered what I thought, in my nervous excitement, was the biggest and most brilliantly lighted newsroom I had ever seen. I took a deep breath. *So this is CBS News*, I thought. I was overwhelmed. The newsroom combined the shops of both CBS Television and CBS Radio. Nervously, I waited for the desk assistant (DA) who would show me the ropes. I was excited by the smell of the newsroom, the clacking of the wire machines, and the voices of writers and correspondents shouting out assignments and breaking news developments.

The job of DA at CBS Radio was roughly the equivalent of a copyboy at a newspaper. My hours were 5:00 p.m. to 1:00 a.m. with Tuesdays and Wednesdays off. The DA on duty took me around the storied news operation, showing me the wire room where at least twenty teletype machines constantly spewed out reports from the two giant news services, the Associated Press (AP) and United Press International

(UPI). "At midnight on Saturday, you'll have to change all the ribbons," my DA guide told me, an extremely messy job that left your hands covered with black ink. He also warned, "Don't listen to the rumors that constantly crop up in the newsroom. They are often wrong!" I quickly learned there was always much talk of who was hooking up with whom and who was advancing professionally. Clearly, I was now part of a very competitive universe and I'd need to be careful to stay out of trouble.

On Sunday evenings, my boss was News Editor Marian Glick, the only woman in an executive position at CBS Radio News. There were also a couple of women of note on the TV side. Alice Weel Bigart had been the first woman writer for a network radio newscast and went on to write for CBS television's evening newscast, *Douglas Edwards with the News*. She retired as a producer at *60 Minutes* soon after I joined CBS News, so I unfortunately never had the chance to meet her. Joan Richman began at CBS News as a news clipper for the research department in the early 1960s and rose to vice president. I worked with Joan when I was an executive producer before she retired in 1989. These were just two women out of scores of men in comparable positions, but I was going to become another leading woman in the profession.

That first day on the job, my replacement had not appeared by the end of my shift at 1:00 a.m. What to do? I was tired. Editor Glick said, "Go home. Cary Aminoff is often late on Sundays." I left, feeling a little guilty, and did not meet Cary until the following Friday, when we each worked twelve hours and our shifts overlapped. He was tall, smart, and easy to be with. He had been an entry-level DA at CBS for about six months before I arrived and was impatient to be out reporting. We had dinner several times before he left CBS, and I watched in admiration as he joined UPI in Connecticut as a reporter and then went to Jakarta, Indonesia, as a freelancer to report on the Indonesian revolution.

I began to hear his reports on the radio from Jakarta, the Philippines, and Vietnam, as he rejoined CBS and was now based in Hong Kong. I was thrilled to hear the voice of someone I knew reporting from the Far East. Three years later, in October 1969, Cary was back in New York City, a big success in my eyes and, as it turned out, my future husband. He took me to dinner at a Korean restaurant. I had never eaten Korean food and was enthralled, but I managed to show off my chopstick skills to Cary's amazement. On Thanksgiving, I brought him home to meet my family. They found him warm and open and were intrigued by his stories of the Far East. Six months later, we were married. By then he had left CBS News again, this time to work at a think tank, the Hudson Institute, run by Herman Kahn.

Three months into my DA job, the three male bosses of CBS Radio called me to a meeting in the conference room. I was so nervous. What had I done wrong? Turns out there was nothing wrong. In fact, they were offering me a promotion: researcher for CBS News correspondent Allan Jackson, who delivered a five-minute network radio report each morning on the important story of the day. "No," I said initially. "I am so new. It feels wrong to jump ahead of my colleagues." But they insisted, "You are more than qualified." In fact, when I had applied for the DA job, I was asked to take a writer's test, something other DA candidates had not done. They clearly were preparing me to move on and were taking into account my education (specializing in international relations and television news) and experience as a print journalist, reporter, and producer of a campus radio show and two Syracuse public TV documentaries. I reminded myself of all the hard work that had brought me to the doorstep of CBS News and finally said, "I'll take the job."

Each day, Allan and I picked the topic for the next day. Was I nervous? Of course. I would tell myself, "Calm down." Some mornings when I arrived at five o'clock there was no obvious big story of the day. I'd choose a story, cross my fingers, and, as I did each day, research, update, and write a rough script. Allan came in at 7:00 a.m. and usually agreed with my choice. He touched up my draft and then broadcast it at 9:00 a.m.

Only four months after this promotion, a friend from the newsroom said, "I'm taking my next year at the Columbia University Journalism School. Why don't you apply for my job?" He was a writer in a department called News Film Syndication. Writers used film shot by CBS News in the United States and around the world to prepare news reports, delivering the finished product to CBS television affiliates for use in their local newscasts. My friend cautioned me about his boss, "Be aware, he has never hired a woman." I replied, "Let him tell me that."

Nervously, I took the elevator to the fourth floor, carrying my huge and heavy scrapbook of articles from my reporting days at the *Middletown Times-Herald Record*, my hometown paper, and the *Providence Journal*, where I had worked freelance while a student at Brown and full-time after graduation. The boss glanced at my resume and barely gave me time to explain the scrapbook. "You're hired," he said, as if it were a fait accompli. I had gotten the job! After only seven months as a desk assistant and then a researcher in radio, I had become a writer in television news. It was exactly what I wanted.

I quickly learned to produce news reports. Reporting from New York City, by reading accounts of the story from the wire services and talking to our crew on the ground, I worked with an editor to screen footage that camera crews sent to CBS News. From the raw footage, the editor and I fashioned one- to three-minute reports that needed narration, video, and, when appropriate, sound bites. After doing the reporting and writing a script, I would have a CBS News reporter narrate the script. The report was sent on a five o'clock video feed to CBS affiliates around the country. It was a way for local stations to report national news outside their area and was great on-the-job training for me.

A year later, a writer job opened at WCBS-TV, the CBS-owned TV station in New York City. WCBS was in the same building where I already worked and I thought, why not apply? I did and got the job. Now I was in the big time, working 3:30 to 11:30 p.m., Wednesday through Sunday, writing for the six o'clock and eleven o'clock news programs. It was local news, so most of the stories focused on school board meetings, events at City Hall, fires, or police work. I'll never forget the first time I walked into that large newsroom: Filled with men at desks typing away, I took a deep breath and took off my good luck charm bracelet. I certainly felt like I needed the luck, but I wasn't going to let a room full of men hear the jangling of my bracelet and see me break into a sweat.

One day I was assigned a bank robbery story that was absolutely going to make it on the air. Writers gathered around me at my typewriter as we quickly put the facts together. "The time was 2:30," one said. "Did you get the amount?" another asked. My heart was beating very rapidly, energized by the team sport of journalism. I finished writing the report minutes before it aired.

My next stop would be back at the network again, but this time on the television side. The year 1968 was tumultuous for America, with war, assassinations, and a presidential election. This was a year when big stories were a daily diet. I applied for and got a job on the *CBS Morning News*. The executive producer (EP), the head of the broadcast, was a former Marine who ran a tough shop. When he offered me a writing position, I spoke up about the title: "I thought the job was for producing." He answered, "I have no headcount for a producer now, but I promise, while you'll have the writer title you will be functioning as a producer in the field, reporting stories." He kept his word. On that ladder to your dream job, sometimes you must take a position that does not look like a promotion but helps develop your skills for the next step. Experience is invaluable, and by making it clear from the start that you want to keep climbing the ladder, you can keep your name in the minds of your superiors for bigger and better things.

In television news, a producer has a complex job: researching and reporting the story in consultation with the correspondent, finding the people to interview, and gathering the best video to illustrate the report. The correspondent conducts the interviews and writes the script with the help of the producer. The producer then works with a video editor to mold the script, video, and graphics into a finished report. I had always considered myself a behind-the-camera reporter, as did my fellow producers.

As a producer, I was in the field with the correspondent, cameraman, and soundman. I would suggest the elements needed and the crew would shoot them. Often the crew gathered visuals I hadn't seen, but which made the report even stronger. I was most nervous at the screening, where the executive producer and the senior producers would critique the report and determine if it was air worthy.

For one of my earliest assignments on the *CBS Morning News*, I was asked to investigate why egg prices were soaring. The idea came from the executive producer's wife, who was tired of seeing her grocery bill go up every week. My research noted that flocks of egg-laying chickens had died during an epidemic, leading to a shortage of chickens and of eggs. Economics 101 taught me about supply and demand, and here I was seeing it in real life. Shortage means a price rise.

My next challenge was to turn what I had learned into a story for television. So, I went with a cameraman and a soundman to a large poultry farm in Orange County, New York, about thirty miles away, to film the egg-laying chickens. After that, we visited a Manhattan supermarket to film eggs in the store. The story seemed to be cut-and-dry economics. Until just like in the movies, the phone rang, and the story took an unexpected turn. An anonymous voice said, "Look at the Chicago commodities market because something is going on there relative to egg prices." What should I do, I asked myself. Finish the shortage–high price story or follow this new lead? I chose to take the bait and turn my gaze toward Chicago.

Indeed, I found that the egg shortages and price increases had been completely manipulated. An egg cooperative in Atlanta held a daily nationwide conference call to determine how many grade-A eggs should be offered for sale to keep the price high. That decision artificially limited the supply of those eggs. Grade-A eggs are sold in cartons in supermarkets. Grade-B and Grade-C eggs (whose shells aren't as pretty but whose nutritional value and sanitary compliance are just as good as their Grade-A counterparts) are powdered and used in commercial cake and other mixes. The co-op determined how many Grade-A eggs should be diverted to that secondary market, keeping the supermarket supply artificially scarce and prices high.

The story was critical enough for inspectors from the Chicago Board of Trade to come to CBS, unannounced and uninvited, asking me if I could add anything to their investigation. I could not, but I learned a valuable lesson: Follow a tip even if it seems to lead to a blind alley. Those tips may expose the real story. One of the secret ingredients of my success was an instinct that could sense if something did not feel correct. I always followed that instinct. Find yours, develop it, and learn to trust it.

For almost two years I produced reports for the *Morning News*, although my title was still "writer." I learned a great deal from my older, experienced male producer colleagues. Remember, when I took the job, I thought I was promised the title of producer. But that didn't happen. So, after the third male producer left, I found the nerve to apply for his job. My heart beat wildly as I went to the EP and said, "I would like John's job." The executive producer was astonished, saying, "Women can't be producers." I replied, "But I have been producing reports for two years."

I was so taken aback I didn't make a fuss at the office. (Although, I am reminded by my husband, that I was furious about it at home.) A few months later, that executive producer was named CBS News London Bureau Chief. One of his last acts before leaving was to promote me to producer! I had succeeded. Speaking up about my experience had shifted his opinion. I only asked once but the EP had changed his mind. I had made it, again. I had not given up and while speaking up in that instance hadn't gotten me what I wanted at the exact moment, it obviously made an impression.

Regardless of the type of work, employment contracts, hiring contracts, and business contracts are serious. They define the job, the salary, the duration of the job, and bonuses to be paid. At this point in my career, I realized I had to hire an agent to negotiate my producer contract, just as the men did. My agent asked, "What will your job be?" I was stunned and said, "I'll be doing the same work as the men producers whom you represent." I could not believe the agent could not see me, a woman, as a producer. I was angry and it turned out my anger was justified, as I later learned that my agent had accepted a lower salary for me than men earned, even though I had been doing the job for almost two years. For a long time, women in the producer ranks made a lower salary than men just because we were women. That policy has changed in the news world, though the practice and enforcement of that policy may still need some attention.

In 1971, about three months after I was officially promoted to producer on the morning broadcast, the *CBS Evening News with Walter Cronkite* came knocking on my door. Senior Producer Sanford Socolow (Sandy or "Soc," as he was known) offered me a job as the first woman producer on the *CBS Evening News*, crashing the glass ceiling. At about the same time the *Evening News* hired a male African American as a producer.

Sandy and the other top producers of the broadcast, all male, worked in a glass-enclosed office known as the Fishbowl. And as anyone who has had a fish knows, the real story is going on inside the glass.

Socolow was quoted in January 2005 as saying, "There was some pressure in those days, with feminism gaining attention, to bring more women into positions on and off camera, but I felt we didn't have to compromise standards one bit with Linda Mason. She's the kind of journalist who makes you proud to have been the one who hired her."

I am exceedingly grateful that I had this kind of support, and I encourage young professionals to seek out this kind of positive backing. And if you're not getting it where you're working, why is that?

During five years at CBS, I had held five jobs. I thought I'd finally landed where I wanted to be forever. How did I achieve this, I asked? I have done the best I could at each job assigned, no matter how small, no matter how long it took, and no matter how complex. And, of equal importance if I didn't understand something, I asked. Of course, I was very fortunate to work with (mostly) men who appreciated what I did. Increasingly I worked with accomplished producers who, on occasion, would share the tricks of the trade. Some tricks I learned by myself. Experience is the best teacher, after all—and that includes what you learn from failures as much as successes.

In the 1970s, the *CBS Evening News with Walter Cronkite* was the number one evening news broadcast in network television, with a huge lead over NBC and ABC. My colleagues at the *Evening News* felt it was the best job in broadcast news. One of them said, "Being a producer on this broadcast is akin to clerking for a Supreme Court justice." I agreed. I was particularly pleased when my male colleagues asked, "What is the woman's point of view on this subject?" Many times, my view was the same as theirs. But on one occasion, the *Evening News* did a report on the changing social mores allowed by the birth control pill. It was a breezy, style piece with no mention of the possible risk of the pill. A good friend of mine had had a stroke at age twenty-three from using the pill, and the flippancy of the report offended me.

I went to my bosses and suggested I produce a report that dealt with the potential dangers of the pill. It became two segments—you couldn't talk about the dangers of the pill without comparing it to the dangers of pregnancy itself, as well as to the dangers of other methods of birth control. Planned Parenthood was running demonstrations of those methods of contraception, which could be filmed to explain how to use each one and the possible dangers. My heart beat rapidly as I screened the two parts with *Evening News* senior producer John Lane, a devout Catholic, who went to Mass every morning. We finished the screening and he said, "You didn't think I'd approve this, did you?" I shook my head while saying, "No." "But I do," he said. So, it aired. A solid victory for a woman's responsibility to tell the whole story.

In March of 1981, there was a changing of the guard at the *CBS Evening News*. Walter Cronkite retired and Dan Rather inherited his mantle as anchor. By the end of that year, there was a new executive producer as well, Howard Stringer, a Welsh-born, naturalized American citizen. He "is credited," wrote the *New York Times*, "with changing the style and focus of the *CBS Evening News*." And, as a result, he brought the broadcast back to number one in the evening news race.

As a newly promoted senior producer, I was able to watch Stringer's magic firsthand. He loosened the broadcast by asking correspondents to appear on camera early in their report so the viewers could see them, adding a feeling of intimacy to the reporting. Stringer had a great sense of humor and loved to have fun. The Fishbowl was no longer a tense place. He was an accomplished writer and editor and scripts became more conversational, which the audience valued. I learned from Howard how to make reports more interesting and how to structure a broadcast. This was valuable knowledge when I became an executive producer myself.

Stringer moved up, becoming president of CBS News and later of the CBS Broadcasting corporation. He left CBS for Sony Corporation, becoming chairman of the giant multinational company in 2005. In 1999 he was knighted by Queen Elizabeth, but Sir Howard says his days as executive producer of the *CBS Evening News* was "a wonderful period of my life and looking back on it, the happiest."

# 4

# THE MOST TRUSTED
# MAN IN AMERICA

I was driving home from the CBS Broadcast Center one Friday evening in the summer of 2009 when my cell phone rang. I quickly grabbed it and a man's voice said, "7:42." I was puzzled and tried to think of an airplane model with that number. Nothing came to mind. "Who is this, please?" I asked. "Chip" was the response. "He died at 7:42." I breathed a heavy sigh. "I am so sorry, Chip." Chip was the son of Walter Cronkite, and for the past week we had been monitoring his father's rapidly declining health.

This was, of course, a tragedy for the Cronkite family and a personal loss for me, but it was also a major national news story. The most famous television news anchor of all time had died from cerebrovascular disease at the age of ninety-two on July 17, 2009.

I got off the phone immediately and pulled off the highway. I was now a senior vice president at CBS News and had important calls to make—to our newsroom, to locate anchor Katie Couric, who would break the news to the nation; to the president of CBS corporation; and to the representatives of the other networks. They had graciously agreed earlier in the week to allow CBS to report Cronkite's death first. I raced back to the Broadcast Center and into Control Room 47 to prepare for our special report.

I had been in contact with Cronkite for the past twenty-eight years, since he left the anchor chair, including the production of a two-hour documentary on his life and times, but it was not the same as working with him daily, which I had done for nearly ten years.

It was long before cable television and the Internet would drastically change the media landscape. In the 1960s, Americans got their news from the three commercial television networks—CBS, ABC, and

NBC—from the Public Broadcasting Service, PBS, and from radio and newspapers. Cronkite became anchor of the *CBS Evening News* broadcast in April of 1962, and by the end of the decade, he had overtaken NBC's popular *Huntley-Brinkley Report* in the ratings, making the *CBS Evening News* the number-one network newscast through the 1970s and into the 1980s.

Today, Cronkite is something of a mythical figure whose authoritative delivery was sometimes described as the "voice of God." But working with him throughout the 1970s, he was no myth. He was a tough newsman who directed his staff to produce the best newscasts possible. And he earned the respect of the nation. Walter was perceived as honest, forthcoming, and wise. And, in the worst of times, reassuring. In a 1972 poll, he was named "the most trusted man in America," and the moniker stuck.

For millions of Americans, the first reports of the assassination of President John F. Kennedy on November 22, 1963, came from Walter Cronkite. And in the days leading up to the president's funeral, Cronkite's somber reporting helped steady a nation overcome by grief and fear. Television brought the nation together as never before. Network news, which had emerged only fifteen years before, had come of age.

Like everyone who lived through those dark days in 1963, I remember where I was when the news broke, a senior at Brown University. I ran from the street to my dorm to join classmates around a black-and-white TV, tuned to CBS. The initial word was that three gunshots were fired at Kennedy's motorcade. We all hoped and prayed that the president had survived. Then we watched as Cronkite ad-libbed, "From Dallas, Texas, the Flash, apparently official. President Kennedy died at one p.m. central standard time." He took off his glasses, looked at the clock, and said, "Two p.m. eastern standard time." There was a momentary silence as Cronkite visibly collected himself, cleared his throat, and continued, "Vice President Lyndon Johnson has left the hospital in Dallas . . . presumably he will be taking the oath of office shortly and become the thirty-sixth president of the United States."

In the following days, we witnessed the power of television to bring the nation together in times of tragedy and trauma. It was then that I decided to switch from print journalism to the immediacy of broadcast journalism. Reading a news story, you had to imagine the scene, but seeing a TV report brought you directly into the scene.

Cronkite also helped reassure the nation after the assassinations of civil rights leader Dr. Martin Luther King Jr. and Senator Robert Kennedy. He also guided viewers through the entire Vietnam War—the first war to be televised right into people's homes.

After North Vietnam's apparent victory in the TET campaign in February 1968, Cronkite chose to leave the anchor desk and go to Vietnam to see firsthand the state of the war-torn country. Walter returned feeling that the war was at a stalemate. For the first time, he departed from his role as objective newsman to share his opinion. "It is increasingly clear to this reporter," he said, "that the only rational way out . . . will be to negotiate, not as victors, but as an honorable people who lived up to their pledge to defend democracy and did the best they could."

President Lyndon Johnson had already started to doubt the rosy Vietnam picture the military was painting. Privately, he was considering whether he should abandon his bid for reelection. A month later, a friend and I were on a Sunday-evening flight headed for a vacation in Puerto Rico when Johnson went on national television to make a bombshell announcement. We read about it the next morning in the San Juan newspapers and thought, at first, it was an April Fool's joke as it was April 1. Johnson said, "I shall not seek, and I will not accept, the nomination of my party for another term as your president."

Cronkite loved the US space program and became a pioneer in space reporting. He avidly read everything he could about space and space travel, and his self-designed course allowed him to interact with the astronauts almost as if he were one of them. Because of Cronkite's own knowledge and enthusiasm, CBS News was far ahead of the other networks in space coverage. Remembering Neil Armstrong's first steps on the moon in 1969, Cronkite said, "I was speechless!" He later added, "I had as much time to prepare for that landing as the space program did. I had watched it from the beginning. . . . And yet when the astronauts landed, I could only say, 'Oh, boy!'" Longtime ABC News correspondent Ted Koppel said, "You could see the excitement in his face. When Walter rejoiced over man landing on the moon, America rejoiced with him."

For all Cronkite's fame and accomplishments, he was very modest. I saw that firsthand when I was in Los Angeles covering California's Democratic presidential primary in 1972. Cronkite was to interview two contenders the same evening—Senators George McGovern of South Dakota and Hubert Humphrey of Minnesota, the former vice president who had lost the presidential race to Richard Nixon in 1968. During the break, I took Cronkite to dinner, making the reservation in my name, not his. He and I joined the long line outside Trader Vic's, and he never once suggested we use his fame to cut ahead. When the maître d' finally came out and spotted Cronkite, we were ushered right in. Oops! I realized my mistake. Why hadn't I put the reservation under his name? No matter. He never said a word.

Walter began his reporting career at UPI (United Press International) from the World War II battlefield trenches in North Africa and Europe. As one of America's top wire service and radio correspondents, he often covered stories from the front. In one case, he landed in a glider with the 101st Airborne to cover the battle of the Bulge. It turned out to be the last major Nazi offensive of World War II, a battle that presaged the end of the war.

On the strength of his war reporting, Cronkite was offered a job, at double his paycheck, by Edward R. Murrow, the legendary CBS News correspondent. But Cronkite stayed with UPI, because he did not think CBS was delivering the news as well or to as many listeners as he was. Murrow never forgot this rejection. Cronkite's biographer, Douglas Brinkley, noted, "Several years later he accepted another offer from CBS News. He came independently and rose independently. He and Murrow were never close."

In April of 1962, Cronkite became anchor of the fifteen-minute evening news broadcast that had been airing on CBS Television since 1948. In 1963, the program doubled in length, becoming the first half-hour evening news broadcast on network television, and was renamed the *CBS Evening News*. I have been told that Cronkite wanted the *Evening News* to be an hour as was true of the *MacNeil Report* on PBS but he was turned down.

In the fall of 1971, I was proud but terrified, to become the first female producer on the *CBS Evening News*, then the nation's number one news broadcast. For the first few weeks, I observed as any newcomer would, before producing my own reports. I was feeling great. A few months later, I was brought down to earth when I attended Cronkite's famous staff Christmas party and he introduced me to his wife, Betsy. "Betsy," he said, "meet Mary, the first woman producer." I gulped, didn't correct him, and said, "Nice to meet you."

After the holidays came a big presidential election year, with Richard Nixon running for a second term and a field of Democrats vying for the right to challenge him. In February 1972, I covered the Florida primary. I was producing Walter's lead pieces and arrived in the Sunshine State before he did. Walter phoned me and asked that I leave rough drafts of his proposed scripts under his hotel room door. But he cautioned me, "Don't let them be too rough. I've hurt my back and can't be much help to you."

Now I was nervous. I worked on the first script and, in those days before e-mail, I called home at 3:00 a.m. to read it to my husband, who said it was fine. I took the elevator and headed to Walter's room, pushing the script under the door, as instructed. Later that morning, my heart in my throat, I made my way back to Cronkite's hotel room. This was my first report with Walter Cronkite and I was the new kid on the block. Walter deemed the script "excellent." Whew! Then I had to set up the large, to me, complicated, tape recorder. As Walter saw me struggling, he smiled and said, "Give that to me. I've worked with tape recorders for years." When he recorded the narration, the report sounded like a Walter Cronkite original. I was stunned. I learned that one of Cronkite's gifts was to read each script as if it were his from the beginning.

This was my first big story since joining the broadcast in the fall. I did the reporting and learned that in addition to the candidates for governor and other offices, busing was a huge issue on the ballot. I suggested to the senior producer of the broadcast in New York that I do a separate report on the busing amendment. He agreed. I learned that sometimes the story I was reporting had more dimensions than I had first thought. And, in this case, it meant Cronkite had two segments on the broadcast. My advice: As you dive into a story and there is more than was visible in the beginning, speak up. My boss could have said "no" or "incorporate that information into one report." It was a valuable lesson.

One of the next big primaries was in Wisconsin in April. This time, I was the producer who stayed in New York to add graphics and other elements to Cronkite's report from the field. I called his producer in Wisconsin to say some of the suggested script would not work with the elements I had in hand. Five minutes later, Walter called, "Linda, I've been told you don't think the script will work." I swallowed hard and said, "Walter, I just think we can make it better." And then I explained. He sighed and said he thought I was correct and not "because of that women's lib thing!" The incident taught me an important lesson. Speak up if you feel something can be done better. The best of the best demand that their on-air product be as perfect as possible. That meant telling Walter, and in later years Dan Rather and Charles Kuralt, that I thought they could write or deliver their narration more effectively. They always listened. It was scary, given their reputations, but I decided it was best to be honest when I believed doing it my way would have a greater impact on our viewers.

I was in the control room on January 22, 1973, when, for the second time in ten years, in another dramatic television moment, Walter announced the death of an American president. The *CBS Evening News* was in the middle of a filmed report on the Vietnam War peace talks when Walter suddenly appeared on camera, at his desk. He was on the phone and held up a finger, signaling to the audience to wait a moment. Cronkite then revealed he was on the phone with Lyndon Johnson's press secretary, who had just told him the former president died earlier in the day.

Walter had interviewed Johnson at his Texas ranch only ten days earlier. That interview was the basis of an hour-long special that celebrated the passage of three civil rights bills signed into law by the president, the most sweeping legislation of its kind since the end of the Civil War. Walter returned to his phone call and continued to bring the audience details of Johnson's death. You can find the video on YouTube. It is gripping.

Walter wanted his half-hour newscast, which ran twenty-three minutes without commercials, to mirror the front page of the *New York Times*. He wanted our reports to be short—no more than a minute or a minute and a half—so all the news of the day could be told in one program. But he was flexible and gave stories that deserved more attention a greater share of coverage.

The gasoline crisis in the 1970s, caused by an Arab oil boycott, had many suggesting the United States could be running out of energy reserves, especially oil for gasoline. I was assigned to do a quick look at the situation. As I researched the story, it seemed to be more complex and Cronkite agreed. I was assigned to investigate.

In five reports, each running eight minutes, we showed that while sources of energy might change in the future, the United States would not run out of energy. After reading fifty articles that all reported the United States was running out of oil, I found one that raised doubts about this prophecy and noted that the United States was blessed with large reserves of oil, natural gas deposits, coal, and atomic energy. Also, fracking, wind power, and solar energy were just being harnessed. I decided to pursue this avenue. I could always do a quick story on rising prices, diminishing supplies, but this might shine a whole new light.

So, while signs at gas stations proclaimed "Gas, Regular Customers Only" and "Gas by Appointment Only" or "Pumps Closed," and customers (including me) sat in gas lines for hours to fill up their tanks, I set out to see if this gasoline shortage caused by an Arab boycott in retaliation for supporting Israel during the Yom Kippur War was temporary or a harbinger of energy disaster for the United States in the future.

We found that US oil deposits offshore were not yet developed. I was astounded at the US reserve of natural gas, again waiting development to be sent to power plants across the United States. America's coal reserves seemed limitless, although phasing out of this fuel had begun since it was so damaging to the atmosphere. Nuclear power was being developed, as were solar power and wind power. We visited all these sites with cameras to show what these resources were and how they were mined.

In another investigation, we reported that six grain companies had conducted a scam, overcharging the US government hundreds of millions of dollars. Cronkite had gotten a tip this was happening, and the investigative unit was assigned to the case. It was a tough story to crack since much of it was economic analysis. We hired an accounting firm to help us unravel how the six great grain companies of the world played the US wheat subsidy system to their advantage. More than 130 million dollars' worth of taxpayer monies had been siphoned off. The first of the three reports ran ten minutes, as we shared the stories of wheat farms and granaries and the price of bread at the store. The second and third parts illustrated how the payment scam worked. That series won an Emmy.

Walter also looked to the future. As early as 1970, he saw the coming climate crisis. He organized a special unit to concentrate on exploring the topic "Can the World Be Saved?" The series ran for nearly ten years. The eight-minute reports presciently focused on many of the environmental crises we contend with today: mercury-poisoned fish, the release of millions of tons of sulfur dioxide into the atmosphere, towering garbage dumps choking the land, and the Everglades dying.

In 1972, the country faced a scandal at the highest levels of government. President Richard Nixon and his associates were accused of committing political dirty tricks. On June 17, men hired by the Republican Party broke into Democratic National Committee headquarters at the Watergate Hotel in Washington.

For months, *Washington Post* reporters Bob Woodward and Carl Bernstein investigated the crime and the cover-up. At first, the story got little national attention. CBS was the first network to give Watergate serious examination.

Stanhope Gould, a distinguished CBS producer, worked with Cronkite on two long, detailed reports explaining the scandal. The first ran fourteen minutes on a Friday *Evening News* broadcast in October 1972, shortly before the presidential election. Over the weekend, the Nixon White House put pressure on CBS chairman William S. Paley, and Monday's second report was shortened to eight minutes. But the two reports changed press coverage of Watergate. The national press jumped aboard. Nixon won reelection, but Watergate soon became an exploding national story leading to Nixon's resignation.

In that 1972 election year, a poll was taken to measure the trustworthiness of political candidates. Though Cronkite was not running for anything, his name was included in the poll. He came out on top and soon became known as "the most trusted man in America."

Soon after this, I joined the newly created *Evening News* investigative unit, charged with reporting on Watergate as well as another scandal, this one at CBS News. But along with success came setbacks.

Several years later, after I had been promoted to senior producer on the broadcast, the executive producer and the three other members of the senior staff—all men—were invited to a front-office meeting with a CBS corporate vice president. Just the men. Long before the phrase came to define a movement to empower women, I wondered, why not "me too?" Why was the only woman senior producer specifically told not to attend?

My colleagues were shocked and so was I. After the meeting they came to see me. "I'm sorry you weren't there," Dan Rather said. "There was nothing you could not know." The others agreed and said, "The point of the meeting was to share new policies the corporation is adopting."

The next day, the vice president who had excluded me from the meeting came to the Fishbowl, where I now worked with the three other men senior producers and the male executive producer. The room suddenly got very quiet. I realized the awkwardness of the situation, so I walked over and shook the vice president's hand, diffusing the tension. I felt deep pleasure in doing so, though I seethed inside.

# 5

## STANDARDS

## The Secret Sauce

Before continuing my journey, this seems a good place to pause and share with you the bedrock of news reporting, the standards. I consider standards the heart and soul of reporting. It ensures that facts are gathered in the correct manner and the report is based on those facts. The aim is to share facts with viewers and allow them to make up their own minds as to what happened. This means telling all sides of the story. Standards are the secret sauce that keeps reporting fair and accurate. I told the *New York Times*, "The standards are flexible and intended to evolve over time. Standards are a way to achieve fairness and accuracy."

Today standards seem to be ignored in many news reports so viewers tune to the channel or publication that presents their point of view. They rarely hear an impartial presentation of the other side. For me, this is a big chip at the authenticity of journalism, which I believe is obligated to tell all sides impartially.

Recently, Facebook published some thoughts from former CBS News correspondent David Henderson. He wrote, "Back in the day at CBS News, we had some reporting guidelines that seemed reasonable and logical. Most of all, the guidelines helped to keep reports truthful and accurate . . . (today) time-tested rules of broadcast journalism (are) seemingly lost in the dust of trying to get viewer attention." Henderson echoes the observations of many other serious journalists dismayed at the lack of standards in the industry today.

Almost every profession has formal or, at least, informal rules of operation. CBS News was the first broadcast news operation to codify standards in a handbook of some fifty pages, ordered by Richard Salant, a lawyer and president of CBS News. In the introduction Salant wrote, "This is as good a place as any to remind ourselves that our paramount responsibility at CBS News is to present all significant viewpoints so that this democracy will work in the way it should work, by the individual citizen making up his own mind on an informed basis." All employees were issued a copy and it was mandatory reading. The other networks followed suit with their own written guidelines.

In the mid-1990s, I was promoted to vice president and was asked to monitor the standards for the entire network. I worked with a committee of veteran journalists to update those standards and going forward revised them on a regular basis to account for changes in journalism—changes like film being largely replaced by videotape, cable channels arriving, then the Web, and now digital twenty-four-hour news cycles.

Standards spelled out the do's and the don'ts of how to report a news story. All sides must be reported so the viewer can make up his or her mind after hearing all the facts. A journalist must keep personal opinions out of a report; only analysts can speculate or share an opinion.

In my day, many journalists did not register with a political party since it might suggest bias in reporting. For years I have been registered as an Independent and therefore could not vote in primaries. A journalist must be purer than pure. Viewers' insights are all that matter.

Standards warn reporters not to tell a subject what to say or how to say it, nor to re-enact an event to show how it happened. Cynthia Samuels, a producer at both CBS and NBC News, shared on Facebook an example of why placing background music to heighten a scene can be unfair. "While (music was) perfect under shots of the sad grandparents, we decided to cut it because it was so powerful editorially in that context that it unfairly favored them (the grandparents). Those are hard calls unless there are structural rules (standards) to stand against the temptation." In that case, NBC standards were rules set in stone and it wasn't a question of judgment.

Of utmost importance to the lawsuit story you'll read in chapter 7, there were rules for editing sound bites. You could not take a reporter's question from one part of the interview and edit it with an answer from another part of the interview to make a more powerful statement.

As standards chief I would screen *48 Hours* programs and *60 Minutes* pieces to make sure they conformed to the standards rules. No surprise, these very sophisticated broadcasts did.

My office was a place to discuss getting the elements of a story and how to solve various problems. I worked closely with the law department, who had advice on how to achieve certain goals. I had years of experience to share. Investigative reports were cleared with me as were all hidden camera shoots. I was always available to discuss standards on an upcoming shoot. For instance, if you want to be taping when the reporter knocks on the door, where is the camera allowed to be? The house is on private property but the sidewalk is public, so you could set your camera up on the sidewalk.

We also constantly updated the standards. Those updates often came after something seemed amiss on a report. One update stated that if the reporter covered the breaking story on scene, he could sign off with the location. But if the story changed significantly before broadcast, the sign off the reporter used should state the location of the recording point. The goal: not to give viewers the impression that the reporter had been at the latest scenes. The whole purpose was that the viewer was seeing what happened. Today, with so many ways to record and edit a scene, the truth can be easily hidden.

Susan Zirinsky, executive producer of *48 Hours,* once told a standards meeting of her broadcast's staff, "If you have a question, calling Linda is a good idea. You might not always like her suggestion, but she is almost always correct."

As an illustration of how important following the standards are, in chapter 19 you'll see how a blatant disregard for a basic standard led to a huge scandal at CBS News.

Blogging became very popular, and for most it was an avenue to express personal opinions. We monitored these carefully because, again, we wanted to make sure that CBS News personnel remained impartial, so our reporting did not take sides.

There was one incident so flagrant I will never forget it. *CBS Evening News* anchor Katie Couric did a radio report each day. On a slow summer news day, Katie's writer copied a *Wall Street Journal* article about public libraries. Couric read the report on CBS Radio as if it were original to CBS. The newspaper called to find out how this had happened. When I confronted the writer, she had no answer for her blatant plagiarism. She was fired.

For me, standards were the heart and soul of great reporting.

Once a year, this was before "zoom," I visited each broadcast and traveled to CBS bureaus around the country where reporters were based, to share, in person, the updated standards. The reporters and producers would meet with me and discuss "how to" prepare certain sensitive reports as well as the routine ones.

In my day, there were two broad categories of reports that aired on a news broadcast: "breaking news" and longer-term reports (or take-outs), which shed background on another story in the news. Breaking news stories were reported from the scene earlier in the day. It could be a fire, a battle scene, a press conference. The correspondent and producer would arrange the report with footage from the scene narrating what had happened, interspersed with interviews of people involved. Those reports were probably one or two minutes long.

The so-called "take-out" stories were an explanation of why or how certain events were happening. I much preferred these stories as it gave me the luxury of time to prepare and report the story. With the help of a researcher, I would read what there was to know about the subject and call people mentioned in the articles to get further information and see if they would be willing to be interviewed on camera for the report. I would select places to shoot the story, call to get permission to shoot, and then head out with the crew.

Back at the office, I would screen the film (or later the tape) with an editor, help the correspondent write a script, record that report, and edit it. The final step was the Fishbowl screening, which could be quite upsetting if the executive producer and the senior producers had problems and asked for significant changes.

I loved doing the research and sometimes found that stories that seemed to be true, were not. See the egg price story in chapter 3 and the America running out of energy report in chapter 4.

Although I enjoyed going out to report, I would often have a queasy stomach each day I was scheduled to work in the field, taping elements or interviews for a story. One day I forgot I had an assignment and I told Cary I had a queasy stomach. He said, "Aren't you shooting that story today?" I was. It was like my mind had forgotten, but my body was still feeling the stress of the day's planned events.

In those days, the producer often drove the rented car with the correspondent as the passenger. For me, driving to locations could be a challenge since I do not have a great sense of direction. For Bruce Morton, a gifted political correspondent from Washington, this was no problem, and we would laugh together if we ended up in some dead end. Certain other correspondents would become impatient when I made a wrong turn. . . . Just added a little tension, which I learned to defuse.

One of the things I loved most was visiting people in their homes to see their exhibits or conduct an interview. Coming from a small town made me feel comfortable with these intimate settings. I was a bit like a neighbor. For instance, working on a story in California, the family invited me, the correspondent, and the crew of three to a barbecue dinner. I said we'd love to, and CBS would pay. We went to the supermarket and the hostess carefully checked the price of each item. At home she carefully measured the amount of meat for each burger, making sure not to waste anything. I felt very comfortable and kept learning, story after story, that while I was from just one small town, I could identify with families everywhere.

# 6

## CBS SCANDAL

### Drugs, Payola, and the Mafia

Reporting the unfolding Watergate scandal sucked up a large part of CBS News' resources in the summer of 1973 as the Nixon administration's "dirty tricks" were revealed, one by one. But in the newly minted investigative unit, we had another scandal to report, this one inside our own corporation. The two scandals were about to collide.

When the Senate Watergate Committee heard testimony that there were Oval Office audio recordings of the illegal activities of Watergate, CBS News demanded they be made public. The White House adamantly refused and asked, "Why isn't CBS News investigating the scandal in its own house—payola by CBS Records?" What the White House didn't know was that the newly created investigative unit was doing just that. We just weren't announcing it.

In July of 1973, the CBS News investigative unit was charged with reporting on the role of the Mafia, drugs, and payola (the practice of secretly bribing someone to promote something) in the music industry. Award-wining producer Stanhope Gould, associate producer Mary Halloran, and I spent the next year digging into the music business. It was a project fraught with difficulties since it shed a harsh light on a corporate division, CBS Records, and on our parent company, the Columbia Broadcasting System. CBS News president Richard Salant promised a "no-holds-barred" investigation, even if it led to the top of the corporation, but when it came time to televise the results, CBS News management, under pressure from the corporation, moved our investigation from three parts on the weekday *Evening News*, with a guaranteed large audience, to a one-hour documentary, *The Trouble with Rock*, airing at six o'clock on a Sunday evening (when most Americans would have been having family dinner rather than watching TV) in August 1974.

Obviously, the network wanted the smallest audience possible. On the one hand, I was furious. On the other, I admired CBS News management, because they could have bowed to pressure from the corporation, ruled the report "old news," and killed the report outright.

Without question, this delicate project taught me how to walk a tightrope when looking inside my own company. It also helped develop my skills as an investigative reporter. Federal prosecutors were conducting a criminal investigation and would not confirm what we had uncovered. I had never been in a situation like this. Since the lawyers in the US attorney's office in Newark, New Jersey, wouldn't talk to us, I asked if we could work out a signal instead: If I gave them wrong information, would they cough? I would then know I was off course, but I could still maintain that I had never been told anything by the federal investigators.

The deeper we dug, the more nervous I became. We were reporting on illegal activities within CBS. The records division had allegedly given money, heroin, and other drugs as "payola" to DJs and music directors at radio stations across the country. In return, the radio stations engaged in a practice called "pay for play," and they would play CBS records more times than other companies' records, thus boosting sales for the CBS records. Other record companies engaged in similar activities, but CBS Records was the largest in the world at the time and was one of the first to be investigated.

Back in February 1973, Pasquale "Pat" Falcone, a talent agent representing CBS Records artists, had been arrested for heroin trafficking. When the police investigated his paperwork, they found the name David Wynshaw, vice president of CBS Records and a close associate of Clive Davis, the president of CBS Records. Wynshaw was immediately fired. He went on trial and spent a year in prison. Several months later, CBS fired Davis, accusing him of padding his expense account.

Almost daily, new details of the payola scandal were making headlines across the country. This was far more than a public relations disaster for CBS, though, this was a criminal practice endangering a large percentage of the CBS corporate income. Corporate management was furious that the news division had ignored repeated requests to stop reporting the story, especially as our investigation became increasingly disturbing. It was almost a civil war between two divisions of the company. The top-level politics of the investigation were being handled by executives at News, and they shielded us as we kept investigating, taking it to the next level again and again. As we gathered more facts, a fuller picture emerged of "pay for play"—a system that guaranteed inflated sales and earned fortunes for the record companies.

We followed one lead to Fort Lee, New Jersey, where we talked to a fringe Mafia figure, an associate of Pat Falcone. We had located him with help from the principal at the Fort Lee High School, who showed us his picture in the yearbook and directed us to his apartment. On the way there, I was less worried about our safety than excited to finally being on our way to our first interview. "What are we going to say, Mary?" I asked Associate Producer Mary Halloran. As we approached the street number, I saw a shiny sports car. "This must be it."

Sure enough, we rang the bell and a man in his mid-twenties opened the door. He was dark-haired, medium height, and wore jeans and a T-shirt. We identified ourselves and asked, "Do you know a former receptionist at CBS Records named Francine who was fired in the scandal?" "Yes," he said. He told us she now worked at her sister's fried chicken stand in Lower Manhattan. We continued, "We know you have been questioned by the Newark grand jury." He acknowledged he had. We learned much later that he had cooperated with the grand jury. "How were you involved?" With that he stiffened. "You'll have to go," he said, quickly showing us the door. It was clear we had found someone involved with the scandal. Our team was proud and relieved that we were beginning to uncover the truth, piecing together incidents from the bottom up, even as we had doors closed in our faces.

We found Francine at the chicken stand in Lower Manhattan. She answered our questions about Wynshaw and his mob-connected friend, Pat Falcone, a member of the Genovese Mafia family. We now realized without a doubt that there were Mafia and drug connections with CBS Records. Falcone eventually stood trial for drug distribution and was sentenced to ten years in prison. Francine was acquitted in the same trial.

Our reporting took us across the country and taught us a lot about the record business. Attending several record conventions (without cameras), we talked with the movers and shakers, learning how the "pay for play" system worked. As we had learned in other investigative situations, sometimes it's better to show up without cameras, which can cause a disturbance. Once the facts are in hand, you can arrange to meet the subject for an on-camera interview.

As you'll read later, I met Morris Diamond, a record promoter, at a record convention in New York City and interviewed him at his base in Los Angeles. Diamond recounted how in the 1950s, "record promoters" visited radio stations, sharing records with the DJs and station managers, offering them money, airline tickets, passes to sporting events, and even heroin and cocaine to play the records. Federal investigators showed that when these "pluggers" offered payments, their records got more airplay and sales went up. Until the practice was outlawed in 1960, payola was an aboveboard practice. It became a huge scandal and the practice was outlawed in 1960. One "plugger" told me, "Back in the fifties, I would write the word 'payola' on my check stubs. It was a legal way of doing business." Given the scandal this practice caused for CBS Records, it's hard to imagine that it had once been a legitimate way to conduct business.

Tirelessly, we continued to establish facts the grand jury was simultaneously turning up in secret. We talked with a variety of people involved in the music business. Among the many people we interviewed, one was in the US government's witness protection program. He had worked with the Mafia on a variety of big money-laundering projects and talking with us could have cost him everything. We scheduled an interview with him at the lovely (and not-yet-famous) Watergate Hotel in Washington, DC. By midday, we were all hungry, so I ordered room service. When the order arrived, I opened the door to let the waiter in with the table of food. My colleague and the witness quickly hid. When the waiter left, they reappeared. "You shouldn't have done that," they said sharply. "What if the waiter had been armed and about to shoot?" Suddenly, scenes from the *Godfather* movie bolted through my head. I was totally naive and offered tearful apologies.

Right after *The Trouble with Rock* aired, we received a letter from Morris Diamond. He was the "record plugger" I met at the music convention in New York City and he had a small role in the documentary. I was puzzled but not worried. What could he want? It turned out he was enraged by a sound bite of his that was used in the program. He claimed the bite made it sound like he was involved in the current scandal. He threatened a lawsuit if CBS News didn't correct the record, but CBS News stood firm.

Diamond sued "CBS News and Linda Mason" for errors he alleged appeared in the documentary. "I can't believe that I've been named," I said to my colleagues. I was frightened and with good reason. The lawsuit would intrude on my life off and on for the next four years as I spent much time preparing to defend myself while working on my other assignments.

In May of 1978, almost four years after the documentary aired, the case went to court in Los Angeles. I was one of the first TV journalists to stand trial. With help from the attorneys assigned to me, we built a defense to clear my name and underscore the validity of our entire investigation.

# 7

# I FACE THE JURY

In the spring of 1978, in the shadows of the famous Hollywood sign in Los Angeles, I was preparing for a starring role in a real-life drama. The trial of Morris Diamond vs. CBS, David Culhane, and Linda Mason. The setting was the federal courthouse in downtown Los Angeles. Diamond, a "record plugger" from Los Angeles, charged that CBS News had allegedly destroyed his career with our 1974 documentary about payola in the record industry, *The Trouble with Rock.*

In his deposition, Diamond said that after the program aired, the industry shunned him. "The various people I tried to talk to, or I would bump into . . . the vibrations told me they wanted nothing to do with me." The next year, Diamond lost his record promotion company.

I had met Diamond at a record convention in New York City when we began reporting the music story, four years earlier. He was a great talker and enthusiastic about the music industry, where he had worked for decades. I flew to Los Angeles to interview him, and we had lunch at the Brown Derby, a showbiz hangout. Since our report was planned as a three-part series on the *Evening News*, I was in the field doing numerous interviews. When it became a one-hour documentary, Correspondent David Culhane joined the team to conduct additional interviews and narrate the broadcast.

At lunch, Diamond told me about payola practices in the 1950s, when it was legal for record companies to pay radio stations and their DJs to play the companies' records, and about payola in the 1970s, when it was illegal but still happening. Now, four years later he accused CBS News of editing one of his answers about the 1950s in such a way that it appeared he was involved in payola in the 1970s, when it was against the law. We had done no such thing and I was ready to prove it. But I wasn't getting much help.

As one of the first network TV journalists to stand trial, I was in uncharted waters and I was terrified. It was a lonely time, as well, because no one at CBS was giving me any advice on how to handle this. I had to come up with my own plan. I started the moment the suit was filed and spent the next four years reviewing our reporting. I reread the script, rescreened various interviews, and studied the notes I had taken to prepare the report.

I asked to see the outtakes of the interview with Diamond. Outtakes are the part of the filmed interview not used in the broadcast. But the archives record showed the entire interview had been "junked" (thrown out). I could not believe it, and then, imagine my surprise and embarrassment when, months later, much of the footage turned up in a CBS editing room. I had sworn under oath in a deposition that the film was gone, and now I had to swear—this time—that it had been found. The confusion did not bode well for our case since it seemed to underscore CBS News' disorganization.

As I pressed ahead with my preparations, I realized there could be another problem—a conflict of interest. CBS lawyers would be defending not only me but the corporation as well, including CBS Records. I asked CBS News president Richard Salant, "May I hire my own outside lawyer, at company expense, to see if I need a separate attorney for the trial?" I was greatly relieved when Salant, an attorney himself, said yes and gave me a fixed sum to consult an outside lawyer. As it turned out, that lawyer believed it was fine for me to use the CBS legal team.

When I arrived in Los Angeles for the trial, I learned that three lawyers had been assigned to advise me: one a CBS corporate lawyer, one a consultant to the CBS Law department, and one a Los Angeles–based attorney familiar with the music business. For the duration of the trial, I stayed at a hotel in Beverly Hills with my husband and three-year-old daughter, Beth. We had relatives nearby, so Beth had a place to go each day, and my husband had business to conduct

In Los Angeles I was able to focus on the case. Every morning, two lawyers picked me up at the hotel and we drove the thirteen miles to the courthouse. Fortunately, the infamous LA traffic gave us plenty of time to discuss the case and plan that day's strategy.

I vividly remember walking into the imposing Federal Court building and then into the courtroom. My heart was pounding, my hands sweating. I was very conscious of being a young woman from New York and wanted desperately to present myself favorably to the jury. Choosing the right suit to wear took some time, but I picked a tailored pink suit with a scarf that made me feel comfortable.

Testifying was more difficult than I had anticipated because the court designated me both a "technical expert" as well as a defendant. That meant in addition to testifying in my own defense, I would be called on to explain technical issues, such as how film was edited in general and specifically how this documentary had been edited. That was the heart of the case. Diamond claimed we had edited his interview dishonestly, making it appear he was admitting to involvement in payola in the 1970s, when it was illegal.

For several days the court was involved in jury selection, as both sides said "yes" or "no" to prospective jurors. There were only six jurors since this was a civil trial. Court procedures were explained and I was designated a "technical witness" to explain the editing process.

Proving Diamond wrong required a "Kodak moment" or two. I told the court, "Kodak manufactures film with a number imprinted on each frame. If two sound bites are edited together from different portions of the film, the Kodak numbers would not be consecutive and you would know the sound bites had been edited together out of order." Fortunately, I had worked in New York with a film editor who was able to put the interview back together in its original chronological form, with the Kodak numbers right where they should be to prove that the answers Diamond gave in the documentary matched the questions we'd asked in the interview. There was no manipulation in the editing process. At the judge's request, I put a pencil through the metal reel and unwound the film. The LA lawyer whispered to me that this made it look as though the judge believed the information was genuine. I breathed a sigh of relief. The jurors watched intently, although I dared only a quick glance in their direction.

When my expert testimony ended, plaintiff Diamond took the stand and made his accusation that the film had been edited unfairly. I was very nervous as Diamond kept testifying. He had a story to tell and was seeking to regain his credibility. But it became clear to everyone, albeit slowly, that the film proved him wrong.

When Diamond left the stand, my LA lawyer stood up and, following the usual procedure for defense attorneys, asked that the case be dismissed because the plaintiff had failed to prove his case. If the motion were denied, I would have to take the stand again, this time in my own defense.

I held my breath as US District Judge Warren Ferguson spoke from the bench. "Mr. Diamond, I am going to speak directly to you . . . because everything else is immaterial in this courtroom the past six days, except you." Then the judge said, "I believe that the big media executives and Taylor (Arthur Taylor, president of CBS Inc.) are financial experts. They are not First Amendment men at all—they all use the First Amendment only when it is to their advantage."

My heart sank. The judge continued, "I think you have been wronged." I all but stopped breathing but I regained some composure when the judge went on to say, "CBS did not in the slightest defame you, slander you or place you in a false light." What a relief those words were. He continued, "The damages if any have been caused . . . by that boycott of your friends in the record industry, unjustly and unfairly."

The case was dismissed. And indeed, Judge Ferguson wrote in the "findings of fact," a month after the trial ended, that "Plaintiff (Morris Diamond) had not been misrepresented in the News special and his statements were not distorted or taken out of context therein as alleged." In that report, Judge Ferguson also wrote, "The use of said excerpts in the news special was fair . . . Plaintiff was not cast in a false light . . . The subject of the CBS News special was a matter of public interest and importance and was newsworthy."

I was not blamed at all. I had provided evidence that the judge deemed correct. At 11:30 a.m., after six days in court, the story that had haunted me for four years was over. I could not believe it. I was suddenly ecstatic, and totally relieved!

I joined the lawyers to celebrate with lunch at the Brown Derby, where, ironically, I had had lunch with Morris Diamond when I first began reporting the story. A champagne toast, a delicious lunch, and now it was time to collect my husband, Cary, and my daughter, Beth, and go home. Case closed.

As I sat on the plane flying back to New York, my shoulders finally down, I said to my husband, "I have awakened from a nightmare." Cary simply said, "Good to have you back" and gave me a hug.

Soon after this venture, I was promoted to senior producer on the *Evening News*, which meant I would supervise the work of other producers working for the broadcast. The senior staff of four—three men and myself—shared that glass-enclosed office known as the Fishbowl, which looked out over the Cronkite Studio. I smiled to myself, thinking, *Did it again*—I'd smashed the glass, one more time.

# 8

# WORK AT WORK,
# WORK AT HOME

Ten years after I started my dream job at CBS News, I became a mother. That, too, was a full-time job. Balancing family and career is a major challenge, and in 1975, when Beth was born, working moms were not nearly as common as they are today. I had no examples, neither my mom or my grandmothers or my aunts with children worked. There was no manual for raising children while pursuing a career, so I was going to have to write one for me.

Fortunately, in those days, CBS offered a six-month maternity leave, which gave me time to do some planning. I would be the first producer in the history of the *CBS Evening News* who was also a mom. As I prepared to return to work, speaking up I asked my boss for some flexibility. I proposed that I come in at 11:30 a.m., a couple of hours later than the rest of the staff, and work an eight-hour shift that would end at 7:30 p.m. I would take no lunch hour but eat at my desk. And, of course, in an emergency, I would stay late or come in early. My boss agreed to my proposal.

On this schedule, I arrived home by 8:00 p.m., in time to see Beth and put her to bed. Because I was able to spend mornings and evenings with her, I felt very much in touch with her young life. My job still required me to travel three or four times a year, and on those occasions, my husband, Cary, manned the home front without a murmur. He knew travel was part of a producer's job.

While I cherished every second with Beth, I was relieved that she was delighted to see the nanny who came each day. Some people asked, "Are you jealous?" "No," I would reply, "it feels great. I love to see her happy. I have no doubt she knows I'm her mom." As I navigated my two roles as mother and producer, so did the managers at CBS News. This was a new experience for them, too. Fortunately, they were willing to accommodate my needs as a mom—as long as my work at CBS didn't suffer. I made sure it didn't. Years later, when I left the *Evening News* to become an executive producer (EP), I learned that not everyone on the broadcast was happy about the arrangement; chief among them, Dan Rather, who had become the anchor and managing editor in March of 1981. On my last day on the broadcast, Dan said, "I wish you well, Linda, but I must tell you I had real problems with you coming in late each day."

Dan was coming in very early in those days and did not acknowledge the work I had been doing. In the following years, he and I traveled the world making documentaries. There was no criticism.

The 1980s brought rapid changes in the news business. More and more stories were recorded on videotape and could be transmitted in an instant. We no longer had to wait for film to be processed. The result: More reports poured into our newsroom every day from all over the world. That presented a golden opportunity for me, at just the right time. The *Evening News* needed a producer in New York to supervise the producers and correspondents feeding in their video and scripts from the field. Sandy Socolow, my mentor, now the executive producer of the *Evening News*, offered me the position. He said, "The job is fit for you since you'll probably have to stop traveling at some point." I was expecting my second child, Elissa.

And so, I became the junior partner on the senior staff. I still worked from 11:30 a.m. to 7:30 p.m. but no longer had to travel. When I was home, I was Mom and known as Linda Aminoff; at work, I was Linda Mason and concentrated on my job. As Linda Aminoff I had the same last name as my girls. As Linda Mason, I was a professional journalist. It made sense to me; Beth—and later Elissa—accepted it as normal. The flexible work schedule allowed me to do a lot of mom things, such as driving the morning carpool and attending "tots and moms" sessions. After school plays, I made sure to go back to the classroom with my daughter and spend some time talking about it. After years working in journalism, I knew how important communication was! When Beth learned to use the phone at age three, I told the secretaries to put her through whenever she called. Sometimes that meant beeping me in Walter Cronkite's office, but I wanted Beth to know she could always reach me.

As I prepared to take my second maternity leave, I sensed that the two senior producers on the broadcast, both men, were keeping a secret from me. When I came back to work five months later, I found out what the secret was. I had been demoted from supervising the other producers on the broadcast to producing daily stories myself. That probably would not have happened to a male producer returning from a leave of absence and it was certainly frustrating. Ironically, one of the two soon left CBS and I was asked to fill in as "acting" senior producer. In this new role, I assigned producers their stories, approved their scripts, and signed their expense accounts. I would screen a report and make suggestions and then show it to the rest of the senior staff in a Fishbowl screening. I sometimes missed being in the field, but I loved helping producers make their pieces as good as possible.

I did this for months. Then one day, the senior producer who was second in command on the broadcast said, "You're doing a wonderful job." Without thinking, I blurted out something that had been on my mind, "I would like the title of senior producer since I'm doing the work. I feel I have earned it." He looked quite surprised, saying, "There have always been only two senior producers on the *Evening News.*" I swallowed hard and said, "But I am asked to send people off to cover the news day and night, all over the world. I also approve their expense reports. I've earned a promotion." "Don't know if we can do this," he said. "Then," I said very directly, "maybe I'll have to look elsewhere," to which the senior producer replied, "I can't imagine CBS News without Linda Mason."

Several weeks later, I was, in fact, promoted to senior producer and, for the first time, there were three seniors on the broadcast. I had learned something critical. When you have done an excellent job and feel you have earned a promotion in title or pay, speak up. If you don't, your bosses may think you are satisfied with what you are doing and may even take you for granted. That is true regardless of your gender or race. Sometimes you must rock the boat. When someone tells you "There never has been" don't accept it to mean "there never can be." Make your case as I did and change the status quo.

In the fall of 1986, I was offered another promotion—this one meant leaving Dan Rather and the Monday through Friday *Evening News*, and it posed a family dilemma. I was asked to become executive producer of the weekend editions of the *CBS Evening News* and the *CBS Sunday Night News*. That meant I would be in charge of the half-hour broadcasts on Saturday and Sunday evenings as well as a fifteen-minute broadcast late Sunday night.

In trying to entice me to take the job, CBS News president Van Gordon Sauter said, "You've done separate stories that fit into a program, you've supervised other producers' reports. If those reports are like patches on a quilt, wouldn't you want to make the whole quilt?" I resisted at first, since I loved what I was doing. And while it was a huge promotion, I would have to work Saturday and Sunday, which was family time with the girls.

How would we do this? "We'll find our way," my husband said. With his support, I took the job and a wonderful thing happened. My husband and two daughters, then ages eight and twelve, became a superb team. I was thrilled. We all were. While working women must struggle to have everything, I learned again, with a generous partner, unexpected vistas open wide.

I was off Mondays and Tuesdays, so when Beth and Elissa came home from school on those days, I was there. It meant we could go to appointments or go shopping together. I was also available when Beth needed an adult in the car to practice for her driving test. Years later, I asked my daughters if my work schedule and travel had bothered them. They both said "No."

Cary was very busy on weekends. The girls remember him making lunch and laboring carefully over salami sandwiches. Elissa remembers going to wake him up on weekends, since he had to drive her to the barn for lessons and practice. I knew Elissa was an equestrian, but imagine my shock when I attended my first horse show and Elissa and her horse jumped over a three-foot-high bar. My heart was in my throat. Did I regret not being there for the beginning of her training? No, her dad had been. But I was enormously proud of what she was achieving.

Our family ties meant so much to us; we tried to have dinner together as much as possible. Mondays and Tuesdays were easy, I was home. The rest of the week was different. The girls would eat together.

Then, very often, they joined Cary and me later for dessert. My house-keeper made dinner for the girls, but I often cooked for my husband and myself. During the week, I was home in time to help with homework or talk about the events of their day. Beth remembers me helping her with earth science. When we visited the Grand Canyon, she proudly used what she had learned to explain the layering of the rocks to us.

A year after I became an executive producer, I was asked to take responsibility for a fourth weekend broadcast, the iconic *Sunday Morning* with Charles Kuralt. I was the first, and still the only EP—man or woman—to oversee two separate staffs running four different broadcasts. It was a huge challenge, Sunday especially. *Sunday Morning* aired at 9:00 a.m., *Sunday Evening News* at 6:30 p.m., and the *Sunday Night News* at 11:00 p.m. It was a very long day.

My weekends were jam-packed, but it was important work and Cary understood. He had once worked for CBS News so there was no need to explain when I was late getting home or had to go in to work early. The closeness of our family helped give me peace of mind and confidence that I could be a good wife and mom as well as a successful female executive. A partner and children help keep everything else in perspective. I did not feel guilty about working, but I often felt tired.

Decades later, as more and more women forged careers, there was an eagerness to right the wrongs of a male-dominated workforce. The #MeToo movement, which had been simmering in early 2000, burst onto the scene in 2017, and workplaces changed dramatically.

# 9

# WOMEN'S PLACE AT WORK

Gretchen Carlson became one of the first female journalists to go public with a story of harassment on the job. Carlson had been an anchor at CBS News and then at Fox News. In July of 2016, she sued Fox News chairman and CEO Roger Ailes for sexual harassment. Within two weeks, Ailes was forced to resign. By September, Carlson was awarded twenty million dollars and as part of the settlement, Fox apologized to her. Litigation against Ailes continued even after his accidental death the following year. The conviction was a bombshell.

Carlson's lawyers had found a way to use her nondisclosure clause (NDC), which unlocked a series of developments and helped spearhead the "#MeToo" movement's viral contagion in 2017. Carlson campaigned for ending contract NDCs that prevented employees from naming alleged harassers. Finally, in March of 2022, President Joe Biden signed a law giving employees the ability to go to court and name names in pursuing sexual misconduct claims. It had been a six-year battle, led by Gretchen Carlson for the benefit of all workers, not just women.

Protests continue today by women and minorities to advance their positions in journalism and other fields, including medicine, law, and science. Today there are many more women and people of color reporting and anchoring television news broadcasts, although there is much more to be done in all professions to even the playing field. This is one of the huge benefits of the #MeToo movement.

I have frequently been asked to reflect on my experience as a woman in a "man's profession," especially considering the allegations and convictions of men from the broadcast world.

When I joined CBS News in 1966 as a low-ranking desk assistant (DA), equivalent to a copyboy at a daily newspaper, I had no idea that there was a "woman's" place in the newsroom and no idea that that place was far down the ladder. I was one of two women desk assistants in radio, and the other woman performed traditional secretarial duties. In retrospect I came to see that she was performing the "woman's role," while I was trying very hard to do what the men around me were doing. It certainly helped that since my shift was 5:00 p.m. to 1:00 a.m., I was not sent into less-than-safe streets after dark to buy coffee and snacks for the men writers and producers.

Four months after being hired, my bosses offered me a promotion to "researcher" for radio commentator Allan Jackson, who delivered a daily 9:00 a.m. report on the big story of the day. I next worked as a writer in the CBS Syndication Department for several years alongside two other men writers. Because of the mutual respect the writers and I built together, they protected me from the harassment that pervaded the newsroom. I would hear things, but I must admit that I have a selective memory and seem to remember only the positive. Also, I was naive and, I know I was lucky.

I do remember a few times that I felt a man was coming on strong and acting inappropriately. I deflected the advance by indicating I was not interested. Thankfully it went no further. Back then I assumed this was the way it was. Men made advances and women could choose whether to participate. Now, I am sure that some women were unable to ignore these advances for fear that rejecting these men would hurt their careers. #MeToo and the legislation passed in 2022 are helping women manage these situations. Thankfully, times have begun to change.

Even as more women rose through the ranks of network television news, sexism remained. Female colleagues who were at CBS News in the 1970s have told me how uncomfortable they were when a boss made unwanted advances. The women felt their jobs were at risk. I remember an instance when one executive producer said of a female producer, "She belongs in the goddamn kitchen." That remark sticks in my mind while (I'm sure) so many other instances have been lost to my memory.

When I was in the field, with a crew of three middle-aged men (camera, sound, lights), we worked very intensely often for two or three days recording a report. We stayed at a hotel or a motel and when the shoot was complete, we'd hug and kiss goodbye, like family. Sometimes one of the men would make a pass, but I'd brush the advance away, saying, "I'm here to be a reporter and that's what I want to be. I love working with you, but let's keep it professional."

On location, I was the twenty-something female producer, and the person in charge. I knew this and so did the middle-aged all-male camera crew, but I still had to figure out how to make the dynamic work. Since I respected that they knew more about shooting a story then I did, it was easy to create an atmosphere of mutual respect. As we set out, I would explain the story and the main elements we needed. I would discuss the interviews and the various scenes I thought we should film. Then, I would invite their comments, which were almost always right on. I encouraged them to speak up if they had other ideas. I made it a point to be a member of the team rather than the boss of it—even carrying gear when I could.

Sometimes, though, I had to stand firm. I can remember one incident in the fall of 1986, when I was the recently appointed executive producer of the *Weekend News*. I had a huge argument with the editor of the late *Sunday News* broadcast. He was much older than I was and for years he had prepared the late night's broadcast's lineup—a list of the reports and commercials and the order of their appearance on the broadcast. This list was then xeroxed and hand-delivered to staff around the building. CBS had just introduced a new computer system on which lineups could be prepared and mailed to everyone involved with the broadcast. If there were changes, as there often were, these could be communicated immediately to everyone. The older male editor refused to use the computer. And after a heated discussion, he left the broadcast. It was one of the few incidents I remember when I had to be the tough boss.

The next year I was named executive producer of *Sunday Morning*, which was a very exciting and an enormous challenge. I would still produce the three *Weekend News* broadcasts and now I had a fourth one as well. With that promotion I was given a $10,000 raise, which left my salary far below that of my male predecessor who had been producing only one show, *Sunday Morning*, while I now was producing four. I was furious when I found out about this, but since there had been huge budget cuts and layoffs six months earlier and CBS was crying poor, I felt I could not ask for a higher salary. Silly me. I found out later that during that same period men received raises. Like many women and some men, I was hesitant to ask for a raise. I realize now that bosses sometimes agree to a raise when asked. And if they don't, they know you are serious. To do it again, I would ask for a higher raise, be less grateful and more businesslike.

On your way up the ladder, I think you should schedule a talk with your boss to see how you are doing and what you need to be doing to take the next step. I would seek that talk after producing something special and I would not repeat it with any regularity.

For me, the salary disparity was corrected over the years as I continued to climb the ladder. But this experience taught me once again the importance of my mantra: Speak Up.

In the new job, my weekends were jam-packed, but I had my family's support. I did not feel guilty about working, but I often felt tired.

My fatigue at fighting for a place at the table only increased as I climbed the company ladder. It was maddening that men in positions of authority could still freeze women out in meetings or decisions. In 2002, after I had been a vice president for nearly a decade, I felt largely ignored at an executive meeting and decided to follow up with an e-mail to CBS News president Andrew Heyward. I don't remember the exact details, but I told him, "What the discussion yesterday unlocked for me were long forgotten or repressed memories of the not so covert discriminations . . . as I advanced up the food chain . . . the subtle ways some of my colleagues closed me out of things and made me feel like an outsider. That kind of mental game was very hard to figure out."

Heyward responded, "There were a lot of things that were routine then that seem almost unbelievable now. I really admire the way you navigated through treacherous and uncharted waters." Heyward was not apologizing for a past that most of us took as a given, but during his time as president, he went a long way to change the atmosphere by giving women greater responsibilities and opportunities all along the employment chain. And although male executives continued to make many of the decisions, I found I was gradually contributing to the decision making.

As part of my job as vice president of "all else," I thought it was important to establish a program to bring minority journalists to CBS News. After all, I had been a minority when I was hired more than thirty years before.

I attended the various annual minority (Black, Hispanic, Asian, and Native American) journalist conferences. Some executives at other networks found such attendance a waste of time, but I enjoyed meeting journalists from across the country. I would give career advice and hear stories from incredibly dedicated young journalists. I knew how important the right training was, and in 2005 I proposed that CBS News establish a development program to identify and support promising journalists of color, two each year. Heyward agreed and asked me to talk to the news director of the CBS-owned station in New York to see if the station would like to help sponsor the program. The response was, "Two journalists a year? There are so many more that need help." I responded, "I know but we must begin somewhere."

I am pleased to note in 2022 the program is still going full steam and several of the participants during my time are now on-camera correspondents or producers at CBS News or CBS affiliates.

In 2004, I was charged with investigating errors in a Dan Rather report on President George Bush's military service that greatly damaged the credibility and reputation of CBS News. I was asked to work with an outside panel to determine what went wrong. The CBS report was declared erroneous. The producer was fired, and Rather stepped down as anchor of the *CBS Evening News*. A former CBS News executive wrote, "Maybe it's time to see a person of the female persuasion take a shot at putting Humpty-Dumpty back together again." I took the remark as a backhanded compliment finally acknowledging a woman could handle a huge crisis as well as a man.

# 10

# WEEKEND NEWS, HERE I COME

In late 1985, I took my place as executive producer of the *Weekend News*. I was now in charge of three broadcasts: the Saturday and Sunday editions of the *CBS Evening News*, with Bob Schieffer anchoring on Saturday and Susan Spencer on Sunday, and the *CBS Sunday Night News*, an 11:00 p.m. fifteen-minute broadcast anchored by Bill Plante.

During the week, I would approve or assign stories for the correspondents and producers to report. After each piece was completed, the correspondent, producer, videotape editor, senior producer, and I screened it in the Fishbowl. It was the final step before approving a report for broadcast.

On my first day as executive producer, at the end of my first screening—a piece about farming and the drought—every head turned from the TV monitor to me. There was dead silence. *Oh*, I quickly realized, *I'm supposed to speak first*. I took a deep breath and said, "Very interesting, but the farmer seems to speak at the wrong place in the report." I knew from my years as a producer and senior producer how tense a screening could be, so I always tried to make producers feel they were part of a team, not out on a limb, alone. The producer said, "Maybe we should explain the irrigation first." And the video editor chimed in, "Then we can use the footage of the pipes earlier." I soon learned that with a little encouragement, my colleagues usually came up with good ideas to address any concerns I had about their reports. Working together, we made the reports better.

The *Weekend News* staff usually took Mondays and Tuesdays off. The news did not. On Tuesday, January 28, 1986—in my first months as executive producer—the Space Shuttle *Challenger* blew up seventy-six seconds after liftoff. Six astronauts and the first civilian to fly in space—a young female schoolteacher—were killed. The tragedy galvanized the nation. CBS News provided extensive coverage that day and in the days and weeks that followed as the spacecraft and the bodies of the American heroes on board were recovered and the investigation began to determine what had gone so terribly wrong. It seemed that almost every weekend, there were major developments, some important enough for us to break into network programming (often football or basketball) to report what we had just learned.

While I was used to running the control room for our three regular weekend broadcasts, breaking news was a different animal. I'd been given no training for live bulletin coverage. I had to learn quickly, on the job. It's called "baptism by fire," and the goal is not to get burned. During these special reports, I stayed in touch with our teams in the field. They told me what they had learned and what they could report. I was in the control room and I would tell the director of the broadcast which reporter to put on TV. The pressure of going live was enormous, but the more I did it, the better I got at making the right calls, keeping everyone calm and managing my own stress.

Major news broke again this time on another Monday, my day off, later in 1986. I was running errands when I heard a bulletin on the car radio, "Mikhail Gorbachev, leader of the Soviet Union, will meet President Ronald Reagan in Reykjavik, the capital of Iceland, this weekend." By total coincidence, I was in the middle of a book by Tom Clancy that had chapters set in Iceland. The part of the bulletin that rang in my head was "this weekend." I hurried home and got there just in time to take a call from CBS News. "Pack your bags. You're going to Iceland to produce the *Weekend News* programs." Whoa! Where to start?

I knew very little about Iceland, and when my daughters got home from school, we opened an atlas to see where it is located. There was no Google, so no way to see pictures of the black beaches and the beautiful mountains among other breathtaking sites. I was leaving that night and the girls helped me pack. When Cary came home, they excitedly told him the news, but he already knew since I had already called him. I would be gone almost a week.

Before leaving New York, I talked to colleagues already on the scene. "What's the weather like?" I asked. "It's sunny, cloudy, rainy, hot and cold—all on the same day," they said. Although that was hard to believe, I packed some of everything and was glad I did; I used everything I brought.

In the days leading up to the summit, we prepared reports about Iceland. The country had a plethora of interesting natural phenomena. Volcanoes heated underground water in the island nation and provided energy for its uniquely powered electrical system. To give viewers a feel for Iceland's extraordinary natural wonders, we produced an essay on the rugged mountains, black beaches, and geysers. It was hard to pick and choose the reports since there were so many interesting facts and so little time to prepare them.

The summit—the second between Reagan and Gorbachev—was scheduled to run a day and a half, October 11 and 12, 1986; two sessions on Saturday and one on Sunday. But Reagan and Gorbachev came so close to an agreement that an impromptu fourth session was scheduled for Sunday afternoon at 3:00 p.m. (11:00 a.m. eastern time). Great hope had been placed on the outcome of the summit for a nuclear arms agreement. It wasn't to be. Nearly seven hours later, as we were getting ready to go on the air with the *Evening News*, Correspondent Bill Moyers ran up to the set we had built in Reykjavik. The lights were on. Cameras ready to transmit. Dan Rather was in the anchor chair. Moyers, out of breath, said, "Linda, they almost reached an agreement, but it is now falling apart."

Dan was excited to report this breaking news. And I had no doubts. Moyers quickly sat down next to Dan to report, without a script, "the talks have failed." This breaking news meant I had to re-jigger the live broadcast—rearrange some stories and cut out others entirely while we were on the air so the broadcast would end at its scheduled time. Working with breaking news can sometimes feel like changing a tire on a moving car, but I found the process exhilarating. After all, what is news if not the "newest" developments? Despite all the frenzy, or perhaps because of it, the broadcast won an Emmy.

Both Reagan and Gorbachev deemed the summit "a failure" in that it didn't dictate that both sides would dismantle nuclear weapons. However, it turned out to be a first step in securing protection from a nuclear end to the Cold War.

Although I had been hesitant at first to become an executive producer, I had learned how powerful it is to say "yes" to new challenges. And there was another big one just ahead. I was about to become executive producer for America's favorite TV anchor, Charles Kuralt.

# 11

## THE STORY MAN

## Charles Kuralt

After a year as an executive producer, my weekends suddenly became even more jam-packed. In the fall of 1987, I was asked to take on the additional role of executive producer of *Sunday Morning*, the iconic ninety-minute broadcast anchored since its inception eight years earlier by the incomparable Charles Kuralt. I was now responsible for two very different kinds of programs at CBS News—hard news and feature—and a total of four broadcasts each weekend.

Kuralt was unlike any other anchor. He was rather heavyset and rumpled, a chain-smoking everyman from North Carolina who never forgot his roots. He had an insatiable curiosity about even the smallest subject and loved sharing with viewers what he'd learned in his inimitable style. Early one Sunday morning, before the broadcast, I told Charles I had planted daffodils the day before. He shared with me that there are thousands of kinds of daffodils and pointed me to a catalogue of daffodils. Who would have guessed this *Sunday Morning* anchor was a flowering bulb afficionado?

Kuralt was the consummate television writer of his time. He reveled in simple language and wove each carefully chosen word into pure poetry. He made it look easy, but, in fact, he worked long and hard on every script. I would marvel each Sunday as Charles took a suggested script and magically reduced it to its essence, making it simple, clear, and elegant. In a story about kids learning to ride bikes, the original copy given him said "Each child has his or her own style." Kuralt changed it to "Children develop their own styles." A small change, but so much better.

*Sunday Morning* was the brainchild of Kuralt and founding executive producer Shad Northshield. They envisioned it as the television version of the Sunday newspaper, with news headlines and all kinds of features. Stories were often eight or nine minutes long and covered everything from music, classical and jazz, to exhibits by artists current and past, to Broadway plays, to authors, and to ordinary people coping successfully with problems. As executive producer, I chose among the stories producers suggested in these areas and then assigned and screened them, requesting any necessary changes before they aired. There was an added challenge: Northshield featured a nature segment at the end of the program. No narration, just natural sounds and scenic views, to leave viewers in a peaceful state.

I had first met Charles Kuralt when I was a new producer for Walter Cronkite's *Evening News*. Kuralt did a weekly segment called *On the Road*, which became a signature feature of the broadcast. A New York producer helped shepherd each piece to the air. One week, that plumb assignment fell to me and I was thrilled. I was finally being given an important task.

In the *On the Road* series, Kuralt chronicled America. As he put it, "The strength of the country doesn't come from New York or Chicago or Los Angeles; it comes from places like Shelton, Nebraska, population 1,040." For twenty years, Charles toured the United States in a specially equipped motor home, searching for what he called "salt of the earth Americans." Those he met included a 104-year-old runner who beat Kuralt in a foot race, a man who lived in the forest and made perfect birch-bark canoes, and the best traffic cop in Pittsburgh. Who would have thought stories like these would be so popular on a hard news program? But viewers looked forward to them. Kuralt added a special touch of humanity to the broadcast. I soon realized that this was a perfect assignment for me, a new producer. Charles thought like a producer as well as a correspondent. He covered every angle of a story to perfection. Editor Tommy Micklas worked magic with the film. I was truly a supernumerary.

Now as executive producer of *Sunday Morning*, I was working with Kuralt again and still learning from him. In every story, he focused on detail and character. And there was no writer better at choosing just the right words to go with the pictures on the screen. When he visited Monticello, the home of President Thomas Jefferson designed by Jefferson himself, Kuralt said, "Architecture was his pastime, Liberty, his passion." I realized that writing came hard to Kuralt when he mentioned he was nearly a year late in delivering the final manuscript for his book *A Life on the Road.* He told his publisher, "I will revisit my favorite American places at just the right time: the Florida Keys before it gets too hot; Minnesota canoe country before it gets too cold; Charleston in azalea season; and Vermont when the oaks and maples turn crimson and gold." But time and the seasons passed without a finished book, and Kuralt considered giving back the advance money. His editor told him, "There is enough manuscript in hand to make a book, but it will be mighty short." That jolted Charles into writing at top speed, and he soon finished the book.

Kuralt was so well known for his feature stories from across America that many forgot he had also been one of CBS's busiest foreign correspondents. He once covered all of South America and traveled the world for the weekly program *Eyewitness to History.* When President Reagan went to the Soviet Union in 1988 for his fourth summit with Mikhail Gorbachev, Charles and I took *Sunday Morning* to Moscow. We were able to do that because both the *Evening News* and *CBS This Morning* were to originate from the Soviet capital as well, and CBS technicians could set up a studio for us. We produced reports for the *Evening News* as well as *Sunday Morning.* It was a huge undertaking.

This was the final Reagan-Gorbachev summit. When they shook hands outside the Kremlin, I was twenty feet away and had goose bumps. I knew I was a part of the history they made or at least a witness to it.

I had been to the Kremlin once before, as a college student, participating in the Experiment in International Living, an organization that places students in homes around the world to experience how people live in various countries. I had lived with twelve American college students for two months with separate families in Warsaw, Poland. We were now touring Moscow. I joined a fellow experimenter and we attempted to enter the Kremlin while President Ronald Reagan and Soviet premier Mikhail Gorbachev were meeting.

My heart was beating wildly as we entered the Kremlin doors and the security guards stopped us. While I pulled out my press pass, my colleague brandished a Wisconsin fishing license complete with gold seals. The guards waved off my press pass but were impressed with my colleague's fishing license and all its stamps. After deliberation the guards allowed us to wait outside the Kremlin doors, where we were able to shake Ambassador Adlai Stevenson's hand after he signed the first nuclear arms agreement between the United States and the USSR. I never imagined I'd be back. But twenty-five years later, Charles and I were standing practically in the same spot.

It was sheer excitement to wander around the Kremlin and Moscow with Charles and the camera crew to record his on-camera introductions to reports already prepared about Russian history and art. While walking on the Kremlin grounds, we heard a young girl calling, "Mr. Kuralt . . . Mr. Kuralt." She was an American college student on a tour of Moscow who had lost her tour group. We were glad to help her reconnect with them.

We also arranged to film in a neighboring village. While there, we discovered it was outside the boundaries established for us by the communist government. I gulped as we walked around the village, nervously watching as our cameraman filmed the thatched huts and other small dwellings. "These are white birch trees, Russia's national tree," Kuralt noted, snapping photos of the trees, the food, and the faces of the peasants. We were a total curiosity to them. No Americans had been to their village for a very long time, if ever.

Kuralt demonstrated the power of a small story writ large when he met an old Russian dentist named Dr. Nikita Aseyev. "He was a stocky bulldog of a man, who barged into the hotel where I was staying in Moscow," Kuralt wrote. Aseyev had a story he was desperate to tell, but no reporters would listen. Except Kuralt. We took Aseyev to a nearby park for an interview. The World War II veteran told Charles, "I was a prisoner of war in a German prison camp where eight thousand American POWs had been held as well. For more than forty years, I have been trying to get in touch with the American POWs enslaved in that camp to thank them for saving my life." He explained, "The Americans threw food over the fence once a week, keeping hundreds of Russian POWs alive." Many of the Americans had long since died, but a few survivors remembered Aseyev and watched Kuralt's report through tears. It was a testament to Kuralt's ability to connect with people and recognize a great story where others did not.

Charles and I would be on the road again soon, this time to China. Together we would cover one of the most momentous events of the twentieth century, and Charles's gift for human storytelling would give the world a painfully honest view of government oppression.

# 12

# TURMOIL AT
# TIANANMEN SQUARE

In May of 1989, I found myself standing in the largest public space on Earth, surrounded by the biggest crowd I had ever seen in my life. Tiananmen Square, in the center of the city of Beijing, China, is the size of a hundred football fields and it was jam-packed with thousands of student protesters demanding freedom and democracy from a government offering only communism and oppression. I had traveled to Beijing with CBS News to cover the state visit of Soviet leader Mikhail Gorbachev with Chinese leader Deng Xiaoping in the Chinese capital. But that meeting had become a sideshow and these protests were now the main event. It was one of the biggest stories of the late twentieth century and we were the only major broadcast network anchoring from the scene, although the fledgling Cable News Network—CNN—had a small presence there as well. A *Washington Post* headline proclaimed: "How CBS Scooped the World on the Tiananmen Square Story."

Tiananmen Square means "square of heavenly peace," but all hell was about to break loose there. Chinese university students began demonstrating in the square in April, after the death of Hu Yao Bang, a member of the Politburo who favored modernization and championed the students' causes. These included combating the corruption and inflation that were destroying the Chinese economy. The students also demanded freedom to attend the university of their choice and to apply for any job they wanted.

At first, there were a few thousand demonstrators, but the numbers grew into the hundreds of thousands by the time of the final bloody clash with the Chinese army in early June.

Charles Kuralt, Dan Rather, and I landed in Beijing along with our crews late on Friday, May 12, to cover the arrival of Soviet premier

Mikhail Gorbachev on Monday for a historic meeting with Chinese leader Deng Xiaoping.

In February, after the Japanese emperor's funeral, President Ronald Reagan stopped in China to pay his respects to Deng Xiaoping. So did the networks. But, only one network, CBS News, went back to anchor coverage of the pending Deng-Gorbachev summit in May.

The other news operations were contemplating coverage in Panama, where there were rumblings of a coup against Panama president Manuel Noriega. On our chartered flight to Beijing, Dan was a little apprehensive. "Do you think we're making the right move?" he asked me. I assured him we were and reminded him that on our previous trip here, he and his executive producer, Tom Bettag, had heard from Chinese students that the visit by Gorbachev, the much-admired Soviet reformer, could trigger huge demonstrations.

I was set to broadcast *Sunday Morning* in two days. Our reports about China had been completed. Kuralt and I needed only to visit various locations to tape the lead-ins. On a late Friday night, I was flabbergasted when we reached Tiananmen Square and saw the size of the crowd. As we began taping, we were surrounded by groups of Chinese people who stood very close to us and stared. What did they want? I ignored my concerns when I saw all they wanted was to get a closer look at us and see what we were doing. We were a curiosity. They had seen few white people and even fewer white women. We had to be careful not to appear rude or offend anyone.

At 9:00 p.m., the students were beginning a hunger strike and sit-in that would continue for the next three weeks. The crowds continued to grow daily and began to include members of the older generation who were proud that students were taking a stand for freedom. The protesters knew the Chinese economy had to be reorganized and the ruling Politburo modernized. Now they had a movement. Many held banners: a sea of blue and red, yellow, green, and white waving in the wind screaming "LIBERTY" and "Absolute Power Corrupts Absolutely." Kuralt commented, "The only strength these people have is their numbers." The huge turnout of student demonstrators was powerful. Everyone was caught up in the fervor. It was a time of hope, with a sense of change, experimentation, and creativity. I felt the empowerment and the promise. "I have never felt a wave of history like this," said Kuralt. Neither had I.

Kuralt suggested that for the next *Sunday Morning*, he would stand on a street corner with the crew and record all the protest groups marching by. Thus, he would tell the story of the revolution at the grass roots. That was his great gift; he could crystalize a moment.

After our first *Sunday Morning* broadcast aired, Kuralt and I turned our attention to reporting stories for the *CBS Evening News*. We had a car and a driver. The driver spoke only Chinese; we, only English. There were no cell phones, of course, but I had a huge portable phone with a battery pack that could call New York or the Shangri-la Hotel in Beijing, where CBS had created a temporary headquarters. There, CBS News reporters and producers were working nonstop, led by Executive Producer Susan Zirinsky (who would become, in January of 2019, the first woman president of CBS News). None of us had ever worked this hard. We knew we were in the center of a momentous event.

Our driver could barely navigate a path through the enormous crowd of men and women, young and old, shouting "Freedom, Freedom." Estimates put their numbers at around a million. They carried banners denoting their affiliations: kitchen workers, sanitation workers, teachers, and more, underscoring the huge variety of demonstrators. Amazingly, they remained peaceful and very friendly—lots of waves and smiles—to our car full of Westerners.

Only later did I realize that Kuralt, the crew, and I were some of the last foreigners to walk in the square before the demonstrations began in earnest. Kuralt said on Sunday's program, "No camera lens is wide enough, no reporter eloquent enough, to describe what happened in China last week. It was breathtaking watching people of the most populous nation in the world suddenly find their voices."

Back at our hotel newsroom, we wondered why the government allowed these demonstrations to continue. In retrospect, we realized the government did not want an uprising on the eve of Gorbachev's visit and feared any crackdown might trigger just that. As added insurance, the Politburo moved the Monday welcoming ceremony from the square to the airport. Officials then sneaked their guests through a backdoor into the Hall of the People, which borders the square. They were hell-bent on preventing a riot.

In the days ahead, many of us worked twenty-hour shifts. The magnitude of the story had our adrenaline pumping. I got a second wind, a third and sometimes even a fourth. We reported the story not only on *CBS This Morning* and the *CBS Evening News*, but in breaking news bulletins throughout the day and night. We were the only American network in Beijing. The city's time was twelve hours ahead of New York, so at six-thirty every morning, Rather and Executive Producer Bettag were at the overcrowded square to anchor the *Evening News*, airing at 6:30 p.m. in New York. We were concerned about their safety, but for the first four days, everything went fine. Then on the fifth day, Friday night in New York, Saturday morning in Beijing, everything changed.

Suddenly, helicopters were flying over the square, dropping leaflets warning that the military was entering Beijing. The capital was under martial law. We asked Rather and Bettag to leave the square right after the broadcast, fearing for their safety. Thirty minutes later, they arrived at the hotel's improvised newsroom, where government representatives were waiting. They ordered us to pull the plug on our live transmissions. We refused, asking for written orders. Nervously, I entertained two government representatives who spoke perfect English, while in another part of the broadcast area, my colleagues were talking to other government representatives. We were stalling for time. As we talked, CBS technicians were busy feeding all our video to New York. A half hour later, government officials again demanded we pull the plug. We refused but stood outside and watched as a Chinese technician cut us off. No longer was there communication with New York, but we had already sent all our video back to the States, where it aired Friday evening as a special report. America watched the showdown in Beijing right up to the moment the Chinese pulled the plug.

Immediately, I, the executive producer of *Sunday Morning* and the weekend news broadcasts, and a few other CBS News people, raced for the airport. It was in shambles: newspapers, magazines, trays of food on the floor, abandoned suitcases in the walkways. People were rushing to leave Beijing. We hurried to board a plane to Tokyo, where we produced portions of *Sunday Morning* and the *Weekend News* broadcasts. Whenever a script called for that day's footage of Beijing, I substituted color bars (indicating no pictures) because absolutely no transmissions were allowed from China.

Excellent teams of CBS News producers, correspondents, cameramen, and technicians remained behind in Beijing to continue reporting the story. On June 4, CBS correspondent Richard Roth and cameraman Derek Williams were taken prisoner by the soldiers and were held for twenty hours before being released, thankfully, unharmed.

The crackdown had begun. At first, "People Power" kept the government troops who came from Mongolia and other far-off Chinese provinces at bay. But that changed by June 4. Some demonstrators continued to try to reason with the elite troops to stop their advance. A very famous attempt, caught in a photo entitled *Tank Man*, symbolized the crackdown. A Chinese man stopped a convoy of eighteen tanks by standing in front of the lead one until protesters pulled him out of the way. To this day, he has not been identified. Other demonstrators used buses and their own bodies to barricade the streets. The troops were not deterred. The demonstrations came to a violent end. Soldiers with live ammunition entered the square followed by tanks. No casualty numbers were ever reported, but estimates place the deaths in the thousands.

CBS correspondent Elizabeth Palmer visited Beijing on the anniversary of the crackdown in June 2017 and found that to this day, the uprising in Tiananmen Square is not mentioned in Chinese textbooks or anywhere else in China. The government has erased the students' demands for freedom. And, in 2021, the Beijing government began yet again to crack down harshly on all anti-government demonstrations, including large ones in Hong Kong, which continue today.

**1975. New York.** *Walter Cronkite with cameraman John Smith. Linda Mason on a balcony checking the picture background for Cronkite's on-camera segment. Courtesy CBS/Paramount.*

**1980. CBS Studios, New York.** *Staff of The CBS Evening News with Walter Cronkite. Left to right: Linda Mason, senior producer; Sandy Socolow, executive producer; Walter Cronkite, anchor; Richard Mutchler, director; and Sam Roberts and Mark Harrington, senior producers. Courtesy CBS/Paramount.*

**1981. CBS Studios, New York.** *Senior Staff of* The CBS Evening News with Dan Rather. *Left to right, front to back: Lane Venardos, executive producer; Bill Crawford, Andrew Heyward, and Linda Mason, senior producers; John Mosedale, writer; Mark Harrington, senior producer; Tom Bettag, senior producer; Steve Besner, associate director; Sandy Polster, writer; Lee Townsend, editor; and Richard Mutschler, director. Courtesy CBS/Paramount.*

**1984. CBS Studios, New York.** *The Fishbowl of* The CBS Evening News with Dan Rather. *Left to right, front to back: Linda Mason, Tom Bettag, and Bill Crawford, senior producers; Lee Townsend, editor; Dan Rather, anchor; and Lane Venardos, executive producer. Courtesy CBS/Paramount.*

**1989. Tokyo.** *Checking the camera monitors before a shoot in a Tokyo department store. David Browning and Linda Mason. Courtesy CBS/Paramount.*

**1990. CBS Studios, New York.** *Linda Mason and Charles Kuralt prepare for broadcast. Courtesy CBS/Paramount.*

**1993. Vietnam.** *General Norman Schwarzkopf and Dan Rather wait for cameras to set up with Vietnamese people in the fields of Vietnam. Courtesy CBS/Paramount.*

**1993. Vietnam.** *Dan Rather, General Norman Schwarzkopf, and Linda Mason prepare for the next filming. Courtesy CBS/Paramount.*

**1993. Vietnam.** *Linda Mason checking camera view before filming. Courtesy CBS/ Paramount.*

**1994. California.** *Linda Mason and Charles Kuralt prepare to interview former President Ronald Reagan. Courtesy CBS/Paramount.*

**1996. Southeast Cuba.** *Linda Mason, Dan Rather, and Fidel Castro near guerrilla hideout from where the rebel forces waged the Cuban revolution in the mid-1950s. Courtesy CBS/Paramount.*

**2002. CBS Studios, New York.** *Dan Rather, Linda Mason, and Walter Cronkite as Walter retires from CBS Inc. Courtesy CBS/Paramount.*

# 13

# RATHER AT THE HELM

In March of 1981, there was a seismic shift at CBS News. Walter Cronkite stepped down after nineteen years as anchor and managing editor of the *CBS Evening News*. The "most trusted man in America," who had reported the biggest stories of the past two decades—from the assassination of one president to the resignation of another, from the tragedy of the Vietnam War to the triumph of man's first steps on the moon—was signing off for the last time. He was just months from turning age sixty-five, then the mandatory retirement age at CBS. Cronkite was the only anchor the *Evening News* staff had ever known, and now Dan Rather, forty-nine years old, would be sitting at Cronkite's desk, though not in his chair. They rolled in a new one for the new anchor. All of us on the staff wondered what this change at the top would mean to us.

A few weeks before Cronkite's final "that's the way it is," Rather began to show us how it was going to be. One evening, after the Cronkite broadcast, Rather appeared on the *Evening News* set to rehearse his new role. He was energetic, intense, and brought a sense of excitement. As we walked to the studio, Dan said to me, "Linda, the most important thing to me is loyalty. I expect people in the foxhole with me are willing to take a bullet." I was a bit stunned but answered, "Consider me in that foxhole; but I don't think I can take a bullet. I have a family." Was this all right for a woman to say? For me, the answer was yes. I had given my honest opinion, but I wondered how a man would have answered.

Rather had certainly earned the job. As a correspondent for CBS News, he reported from Dallas that November day in 1963 when President Kennedy was shot and broke the news of his death. He risked

79

his life covering hurricanes, the civil rights struggle in the South, and the Vietnam War. As White House correspondent, Rather went with President Nixon on his historic trip to China in 1972 and covered the Watergate scandal that drove him from office two years later. He had reported all this on Cronkite's *Evening News*. Now Rather set out to make the broadcast his own. He brought new energy to the *Evening News*, coming to work early and staying late. He worked hard and showed his appreciation when others did the same. No Thanksgiving passed without a Texas pecan pie arriving at my front door or a birthday without flowers at my desk. Others on the staff also experienced similar expressions of Rather's gratitude.

As a senior producer, I worked very closely with Rather. Even after I left the broadcast to become vice president and the executive producer of *CBS Reports*, Rather and I continued working together. We traveled to the beaches of Normandy on the fiftieth anniversary of D-Day as well as battle sites in the Pacific to produce two two-hour documentaries about World War II. In reporting the Pacific theater, we traveled to Hiroshima, where the United States dropped that first devastating atomic bomb. The city was destroyed by explosions, fires, and radiation. Untold thousands of the Japanese population were annihilated. It was heart-wrenching to be there all these years later and imagine the horror, but these overwhelming moments strengthened the professional bonds between Dan and me.

Our guide for this Japan trip was retired general Norman Schwarzkopf, hero of the Persian Gulf War, whose forces drove Saddam Hussein's invaders out of Kuwait in 1991. Now, nearly a half century after the bombing of Hiroshima, Rather and the general sat together on the bridge over the Motoyasu River. It was early morning and strangely quiet. There were cameras, tripods, and other equipment strewn about as technicians set up for the interview. Crowds were gathering to see what we were doing. I asked Dan and the general if they would like some coffee. "Yes," they said. I found a small coffee bar. I spoke no Japanese and the owner no English, but we negotiated a tray with two cups, a pot of coffee, sugar, and cream. I gingerly carried the tray back to the bridge. A producer's job sometimes includes producing coffee.

When the cameras started rolling, the two men talked about one of the most horrifying events of World War II, that first atomic bombing,

August 6, 1945. A few days later, the United States dropped a second atomic bomb, destroying the Japanese city of Nagasaki, forcing the Japanese to surrender and ending World War II.

After the interview, we planned to visit Iwo Jima, the Japanese black sand volcanic island that had been the scene of an epic battle that lasted five brutal weeks. It is estimated that seven thousand American and twenty-one thousand Japanese troops died there, and only two hundred Japanese troops survived. To get there, we had to cut through some thick red tape. The CBS News Tokyo bureau chief, Bruce Dunning, shared the distressing news as we waited at the airport. "A Japanese official tells me that our privately chartered plane cannot take off from Hiroshima to fly to Iwo Jima." "Why?" I asked. "Because officials fear you'll leave from there to fly home." In Japan at that time, there were complicated aviation rules for foreign charter planes to take off and land. "What can we do?" I asked. "I have Dan Rather and General Schwarzkopf as passengers." With the help of our interpreter, I asked a Japanese official, "Can I guarantee we'll fly back to Hiroshima before we leave Japan?" He shook his head no. "What if I leave a member of my party as a hostage and we pick him up before flying out of Japan?" Again, "No." "Can I have CBS guarantee a large sum of money?" The answer remained "No." I was nervous: Dan Rather and General Schwarzkopf were not used to "No." Finally, Dunning tracked down a higher Japanese authority who cleared us for takeoff on one condition: Each of us had to promise we would return to Hiroshima before leaving Japanese territory. We made the promise and kept it.

In 1996, Rather and I revisited another war. We flew to Kuwait to do some filming for the documentary *The Gulf War Plus Five*. We wanted to see what had happened to Kuwait in the five years since the United States and its allies expelled the forces of Iraqi dictator Saddam Hussein. The American base, with its tanks painted tan (desert camouflage), was very much intact. And the boulevard in Kuwait City looked much as I remembered it from watching the 1991 liberation on live TV.

On the flight back to New York, we encountered the "snowstorm of the century," which buried the East Coast of the United States. Planes were forbidden to land in New York City. We had to fly from Kuwait to London and on to Gander, Nova Scotia, Canada. We landed in a field that looked like a packed parking lot for planes.

Truck lights flashed as planes were guided to land, one after the other. It was choreographed chaos.

In the middle of the night, Rather and I caught a flight from Gander to Albany, New York. We had only a few hours of sleep in Albany before rushing for the train to New York City. It's normally a three-hour trip, but not this day. After easing out of the station, the train went about ten miles and stopped dead. We were in the middle of a "white-out." I was unable to see a foot outside the train window. Never had I seen snow this thick. "The train is stuck," we were told. Dan turned to me and said, "I'm going to walk." "Are you crazy?" I asked. He got very upset and stopped talking to me. I knew he could be volatile, so while I was upset, I knew I had to keep my cool.

In about twenty minutes, the train started moving again, inching toward New York as Dan nursed a slow burn. We bailed at the next stop, less than thirty miles from where we'd boarded, still more than a hundred miles from New York City. There were no cell phones in those days, so I called CBS from the stationmaster's office. I told the desk, "There's no way we can get to New York City by train today." The editor on duty replied, "We'll find you a driver and a car with chains." They did. As the car passed my house north of Manhattan, I opted to get out. Dan arrived at the Broadcast Center around 4:00 p.m., in plenty of time to prepare for that night's broadcast. The next day, he gave me a big hug. The waves had calmed, at least for now.

Rather went on to do many years of award-winning reporting, but along the way, the *Evening News* fell out of first place in the ratings and CBS and the other networks found themselves in turbulent financial waters.

# *14*

# CBS IN TURMOIL

The 1980s were a turbulent decade for the major television networks. Ownership changed hands at all three: General Electric bought NBC; Capital Cities Communications bought ABC; and Laurence Tisch, a hotel and theater magnate, took control at CBS. The new owners demanded profits, including from their news divisions. No longer was news to be run as a public service, allowed to rack up huge debts. Adding to the financial pressure, the broadcast networks faced new competition from the fledgling cable networks, which provided immediate news coverage at much lower costs. The Big Three attempted to get control of runaway news budgets by "downsizing"—a word that evoked terror. It meant firing employees. And everyone wondered who would be next. Would it be me? My friends?

When Tisch became CEO of CBS in the fall of 1986, CBS News employees greeted him with joy. The honeymoon did not last long. In March of 1987, he ordered a 10 percent cut in the division's $300 million budget, resulting in firings that included fourteen of the ninety on-air reporters and thirty-five of the two hundred fifty producers. In all, two hundred fifteen people lost their jobs. Because of budget problems, almost two hundred jobs were cut in 1985 and 1986. When added up, more than four hundred people were fired in less than three years. Dan Rather said the cuts were driving CBS News "from Murrow to mediocrity." CBS News management called a series of meetings with news executives—vice presidents, executive producers, and domestic editors—to discuss a reorganization. As executive producer of the *Weekend News* and *Sunday Morning*, I attended.

We were asked to determine which employees should go and which should stay. It was an awful task. I fought for the producers whose work I knew. Then, on the day of the "mass firings," we were each given a list of the people to be dismissed who reported to us. We were also informed how to tell them the awful news. We were told to say "downsizing." We were not to tell people, "I know how you feel," because we didn't. The atmosphere throughout the building, indeed around the worldwide network, was tense. No one knew what was going to happen. When I was handed my list, I was horrified. It was brutal. I had to tell ten colleagues, some of them long-term employees, that this was the end. It was one of the hardest things I have ever had to do.

Over the next two years, a total of nearly 350 CBS News employees would lose their jobs as the network went from Tiffany (the gold standard) to Tisch. After leading the way in broadcast news coverage for decades, CBS News was knocked off its pedestal. The *CBS Evening News* saw its dominance recede. One reason: Under Tisch, CBS was outbid by the fledgling Fox network for the rights to NFC football games. That led several powerful CBS affiliates to jump to Fox. *Evening News* ratings never recovered.

The year 1990 began with pressure for still more cuts in the news budget. CBS News president David Burke was forced out in August— speculation at the time was he had refused to make the cuts Tisch wanted. Layoffs—thirty to forty of them—came at the end of the year, this time under Burke's successor, Eric Ober.

I knew Eric well. Almost twenty-five years earlier, we had been news writers at WCBS-TV. Our paths diverged as I became a producer and he went on to hold several executive positions in the corporation. Now we were working together again. Ober decided he needed an additional vice president. He felt the vice president for "hard news" and the vice president for prime-time broadcasts could not cover everything, and there should be a vice president covering "all else." Ober asked me to become that vice president. "All else" meant making sure nothing fell through the cracks as well as being responsible for the standards of CBS News.

I never thought I'd rise to these heights. All my life I had been driven by an inner force determined to make me succeed. I thought I had made it as the executive producer of four broadcasts, but now I was being offered a job that was even more significant, more creative to me personally. Of course, I said yes, and since the job was "all else," I set out to organize it.

Almost every profession has formal, or at least informal, rules of operation. There are correct ways to do things. At CBS News, those standards were codified in a handbook of some fifty pages, ordered by CBS News president Richard Salant in 1976. CBS, as I mentioned earlier, was the first network news division to provide a book of written standards for its reporters.

In the mid-1990s, I led a committee to update those standards, and they have been revised on a regular basis since then to account for changes in journalism. Film largely replaced videotape, cable channels came on scene, then the Web and now digital. Standards are the do's and don'ts for journalists, designed to head off improper practices. The standards say: Do not tell a subject what to say or how to say it and do not "stage" an event.

The news standards require journalists to keep their personal opinions out of their reports. All sides of a story must be reported fairly so the viewer can make up his or her mind having heard all the facts. A journalist must not speculate or share an opinion—unless he or she is an analyst whose job it is to state an opinion. There can be no question as to why a story is being reported. Viewers' insights are all that matter.

My new job included much more than news standards. I maintained a dialogue with the executive producers and representatives of various CBS News programs to share strategies and ideas. I was charged with helping new broadcasts get on the air. I was told to find "space" for the new *Saturday Morning* program. Space? I found out that meant finding office space for the staff. I was also involved with the broadcast's concept, a continuation of the weekday morning broadcast with added cooking and musical features. After the program launched, I met weekly with the executive producer, Hal Gessner, to see what was planned and what difficulties he might foresee.

I helped develop the prime-time broadcast *Eye to Eye with Connie Chung*. It was an hour-long magazine program, created by Executive Producer Andrew Heyward, with interviews, human interest reports, and investigative pieces. I met with Heyward weekly and wrote critical notes after each broadcast. I was involved in the launching of Executive Producer Jon Klein's *Before Your Eyes* series, a highly acclaimed two-hour broadcast presented as a movie, shot cinema verité style, no narration. Both were successful.

But there was a big problem with another program. In 1996 Charles Kuralt retired as anchor of *Sunday Morning*. He was replaced by Charles Osgood, a talented writer and anchor. Two years later, ratings were falling and consequently the broadcast's revenues were dropping. I was asked to help right the ship I had once helmed. Looking closely at the problem, it became obvious the broadcast worked well for Kuralt, who after all had created it, but not so well for Osgood. Osgood had his own special talents, but they were different from Kuralt's.

I told the *Sunday Morning* staff, "Be willing to change, but subtly," and they eagerly responded with good observations and suggestions: "Audiences have shorter attention spans. It is necessary to adjust story-telling techniques. The opening segment should be shorter and snappier." Another suggestion: The cover story should provide a different perspective on a current event, so viewers would return weekly to see *Sunday Morning*'s interpretation of a breaking story. A new executive producer, Rand Morrison, a talented writer and producer, would help Osgood find his voice. Morrison had a keen sense of what the audience cherished and provided those reports. Over time, the ratings went to number one again. Clearly being fresh and current was the answer. It was exhilarating, and all of us were relieved to have the ratings up again.

The most important and rewarding part of my job as a vice president was to act as an informal sounding board for women and minority journalists. It was unofficial, but many people took advantage of my open door. Since I had been a minority myself, I felt an immediate rapport with others like me and was happy to hear personal issues and offer advice. I helped news people think about ways to ask for a raise, how to resolve conflicts with a boss, and how to plan a course of action to achieve their dreams. A common question was, "What do I do next?" I'd explain, "First you must make sure you're doing the assigned job well. Then you can put your sights on the next job, asking your boss directly how you can make this happen." I cautioned, "Don't expect the boss to come to you. Raise your hand and speak up."

When a talented producer returning from maternity leave asked, "Is there any way I can work fewer hours?" a solution popped into my head. Another producer was also a new mom. Perhaps the two could share one job. A job share had never been tried at CBS. It ended up serving not only the two women but CBS itself very well.

I felt it imperative to attend the minority journalist conventions each summer. There I met with viable job candidates, some not quite ready for network news. I proposed that CBS News fund a training program for producers and reporters working at CBS affiliates. The next generation of journalists could learn the ropes from established correspondents—anything from how to stand in front of the camera, to what to say on camera and how to write a script. CBS News instituted the program and it is still running in 2022. Some of the producers and correspondents who finished the program now work at the network or at the stations where they trained. Correspondent Jericka Duncan is based in New York as is Alturo Rhymes, senior broadcast producer on the *CBS Evening News*.

As I took on the responsibilities of my newly created vice presidency, there was still another responsibility to come—one I had dreamed about my whole career.

# 15

# A DREAM FULFILLED

## Documentaries

By 1993, I had reached the highest ranks of CBS News. Back when I was working on the high school paper, I never could have dreamed I would one day be a vice president at the preeminent broadcast news operation in the country. But I did have another dream. And the time had come to make it happen.

I wanted to produce documentaries. And CBS News was known for some of the most powerful documentaries ever aired, including Edward R. Murrow's *Harvest of Shame*. Murrow and Producer Fred Friendly exposed America to the plight of migrant farm workers who worked for slave wages under the worst of conditions. I had been bitten by the documentary bug in graduate school when I made a couple of short films and a half-hour documentary shown on Syracuse TV. I asked CBS News president Eric Ober to add responsibility for documentaries to my portfolio. He agreed and gave me the added title of executive producer of documentaries.

I set up a unit with producers and editors, and over a six-year period we produced more than fifty documentaries. We examined such topics as "Who Killed JFK," "The Murrow-McCarthy Controversy," and "Hitler and Stalin," all subjects that had fascinated me. We visited Cuba and Vietnam, two countries with whom the United States had been intimately involved.

We looked at D-Day in Europe and Victory in the Pacific in two two-hour, award-winning specials about World War II. Visiting those war locations, which I had only read about in history classes, was a nerve-racking experience. Looking at the beaches of Normandy, I wondered how any American soldiers dared to climb out of boats and rush toward the beaches, well-fortified by the German army. One survivor told me,

"I just followed my comrades to the beach." In the South Pacific, it was equally unimaginable. On the tiny island of Iwo Jima, eighteen thousand Japanese soldiers had dug caves in the volcanic island. Only 216 survived. In those same battles, seven thousand Americans were killed and twenty thousand wounded. The rocks and the ocean lapping at the island's shores surrendered no clues to the horrors that had unfolded there.

*Enter the Jury Room* gave America an unprecedented look at jurors deliberating their verdicts. We looked at America's accomplishments in space. And we produced a three-hour documentary titled *In the Killing Fields of America*. Correspondents Dan Rather, Mike Wallace, and Ed Bradley visited nine American cities and documented the violence in each. It won a prestigious Peabody Award (the broadcast equivalent of a Pulitzer Prize) and was widely acclaimed as an unabashed examination of the harsh reality of what was happening on our streets and in our schools.

The documentary unit also produced several hour-long adventures with the Smithsonian Institution to celebrate its 150th anniversary. And we worked with *Time Magazine* to produce three one-hour specials about *Time*'s one hundred outstanding people of the twentieth century.

In 1996, students in big cities and small towns across America entered the ninth grade and would graduate in the year 2000. What would these students bring to the new millennium? I talked with the executive producers of all CBS News broadcasts about following this class from freshman year to graduation. They liked the idea and we worked together to develop story ideas.

The world these freshmen had experienced were the benefits of a booming economy, a wave of school violence, a presidential sex scandal and impeachment, and the rise of the Internet. For four years CBS interviewed members of the class of 2000 to present a portrait of the country's problems and promise as seen through this generation's eyes.

The reports aired on all CBS News broadcasts under the title *The Class of 2000*. I served as the overall editor of this four-year series. We interviewed more than four thousand members of the class. In a 1999 poll, more than half the students told us they thought their lives would be better than those of their parents. Two-thirds were looking forward to a four-year college but were concerned about landing good jobs.

As the new century approached, the media landscape in America was changing and along with it, the appetite for documentaries on network television declined. By 2000, each of the three major networks was offering several news magazines every week: *Primetime Live*, *20/20*, and *Nightline* on ABC; *Dateline* on NBC, which aired as many as three or four editions a week; *60 Minutes* and *48 Hours* on CBS. With our unit competing for airtime and viewers against all these prime-time news programs, I suggested we cut back documentary production and concentrate only on special cases. Andrew Heyward, who had succeeded Ober as president in 1996, agreed. All of us knew we had to adapt to changing viewer tastes. What did not change was the pride we all felt in our work and our motivation to do our best.

# 16

# VIETNAM

## Twenty Years Later

The Vietnam War became known as the "living room war." For the first time, Americans watched a war as it played out on their televisions, at dinner time on the various evening news broadcasts. Through much of the mid 1960s and into the 1970s, viewers saw close-up the horrors of war. TV screens were filled with images of bombings, destroyed homes, innocent civilians, young and old, running for cover, and bodies of the dead. And then they watched as caskets, in growing numbers, arrived back in the United States carrying remains of American service members killed in action.

The war divided the country as no other issue had since the Civil War, more than a century earlier. Some Americans thought it was the duty of the United States to defend an ally, South Vietnam, from communist North Vietnam. Others argued that the United States had no business in southeast Asia. In 1973, a treaty signed in Paris theoretically ended the war, but in fact, it continued two more years, ending only when the North Vietnamese captured Saigon in 1975. By then, nearly sixty thousand American service members had been killed as well as more than 3.5 million Vietnamese troops and civilians, according to estimates from the US and Vietnamese governments.

We had told the story of the war every night on the *CBS Evening News with Walter Cronkite*. Now, in 1993, as executive producer of *CBS Reports*, I wanted to document how Vietnam had fared in the two decades since the communist victory. Retired general Norman Schwarzkopf had worked with CBS News on several projects and we turned to him again. We asked him to go with us to Vietnam, where he had served two tours of duty more than twenty years before. The general said he had strong misgivings about going back and had terrible memories of returning home from Vietnam, years before, to an America where large segments of the public refused to welcome the troops as heroes. It had been a brutal experience for the military and for the general personally. He finally agreed to go back with me and Dan Rather, who had covered the war from the battlefield. We would be away for almost two weeks.

As we prepared for the trip, Dan called me into his office and said, "You know, Linda, a four-star general can be an eight-hundred-pound gorilla, just like an anchor can be. You now have two of us." I became anxious, thinking, *Dan's right! I am the leader of the talent, the producers, and the camera crews.* I knew I would have to trust my instincts. I knew in my gut that if my instincts were wrong and I made a big mistake, I would no longer be trusted with the responsibilities I cherished.

And there was more: The very week we were scheduled to fly to Vietnam, CBS News received an angry letter from three Vietnamese technicians who had once worked for the network. They claimed CBS owed them back pay for work done in 1975, twenty years before, when North Vietnam overran the South. I spoke with CBS News business affairs and was told they would settle the matter. But I never stopped worrying that the technicians might still intrude on the shoot and disrupt it completely.

Dan and I picked up General Schwarzkopf in San Francisco. From there, we flew to Singapore. As experienced world travelers, Dan and Schwarzkopf slept all the way. I was too overwrought, going over and over my mental checklist, to sleep. I wondered and worried what details I might have forgotten.

When we landed in Singapore, everyone at the airport seemed to recognize Schwarzkopf, who was more than six feet tall and broad-chested. It was amazing to see travelers suddenly realize who he was, then quickly look away. It was impolite to stare. He had been in the news often after he triumphed in the Persian Gulf War in 1991 and returned home a hero. His history in Asia was more complicated, though. We caught our flight from Singapore to Vietnam, landing at Tan Son Nhat International Airport. It was quite an emotional experience for me to watch the general and Rather choke up as memories assaulted them.

We drove to our hotel in what was once the capital city of Saigon, now renamed Ho Chi Minh City, in honor of the leader of Vietnam's communist revolution. The hotel rooms were a picture of modernity. They had phones on which you could set a wake-up alarm. That may seem archaic nowadays, but I had not seen phones like that before in all my travels. How extraordinary I thought, this country that needs so much—rebuilding streets and buildings, installing electricity and water—gave priority to modern phones.

As we walked the streets, the general and Rather agreed that Ho Chi Minh City seemed the same as when they had been in the country during the war. There were motorbikes zooming about, but very few cars. That afternoon, we headed for the Majestic Hotel, overlooking the Saigon River. The hotel roof seemed the perfect spot to capture the river below and the cityscape in the distance. But there was a potential problem. A member of our team who had traveled to Vietnam ahead of us warned that some disgruntled Vietnamese wanted to attack the general. So, this location could be dangerous.

Every shoot I had ever been on, even the simplest, had aspects that were unanticipated. Producing means quickly finding a way around any obstacle. I alerted the general to the possible danger. He replied, "Let's go. I'm not afraid." So, we went. But when we reached the roof, I asked Rather's assistant to use his personal camera to scan all the buildings surrounding the hotel, to make sure there was no sniper position from which to take a shot at the general. Thankfully we were safe. What a great relief when our twenty minutes of taping were over!

The next day we traveled about an hour and a half north of Ho Chi Minh City to Cu Chi, where we explored the elaborate tunnel system dug by communist Viet Cong guerrillas during the war. Those tunnels, more than two hundred miles of them, were used to transport food, water, and munitions and are now preserved for all to see. In the rest of the country, hundreds of miles of tunnels had been dug during the French occupation. Troops, food, and ammunition moved down the "Ho Chi Minh Trail," the military supply route that ran from the communist North through Laos and Cambodia to the South. Those tunnels also allowed the North Vietnamese to launch surprise attacks on American troops. As we inspected some of the tunnels, we noted how each had been dug very deep, very low and narrow, and so small that a person could barely enter the tunnel and move around. Of course, the Vietnamese had much smaller physiques than the American

GIs. It was amazing a person could enter the tunnel and move around! Today, all was eerily silent.

The next day we flew more than five hundred miles north of Ho Chi Minh City to the port city of Danang, on the South China Sea. We had to travel by helicopter, since roads were treacherous. The general had clearly stated, "I won't fly in a Russian plane," and I thought I had secured the only non-Russian aircraft in Vietnam—a Puma (Italian) helicopter. But on the runway, my heart started to beat wildly when I suddenly saw Russian writing on the chopper. Fortunately, no one else noticed, or if they did, no one said a word about it. We boarded and headed to Danang.

The landing zone was on a barren hilltop, overlooking the scene of a major battle that continued to haunt the general. You could see him physically brace himself as memories overtook him. Twenty years ago, as a lieutenant colonel, he had flown by helicopter to this battlefield, which the enemy had thoroughly mined, thereby trapping a US platoon. Some Americans were dead, others frozen in fear. Schwarzkopf landed his helicopter and took charge. He rescued a soldier wounded in the minefield and carried him out of danger. He sent that soldier and other wounded soldiers back on his helicopter. He remained behind, sustaining gunshot wounds himself. All these years later, as Rather interviewed the general, the crew and I could feel the tension of those terrible memories. Under intense self-control, Schwarzkopf showed no emotion, although his terror was palpable to those of us on the hill.

In the middle of the interview, we were astonished to see that more than fifty Vietnamese had climbed the hill to check us out. The villagers hadn't seen white people for decades, and a white woman was a shock. One of our two "minders," sent by the communist government to accompany us, observed, "these peasants are not too smart. No one wears glasses and that must be because no one reads." It was clear that these North Vietnamese government representatives felt superior to the South Vietnamese locals. Neither Dan nor Schwarzkopf was surprised by their comments.

We returned to Ho Chi Minh City and I faced another, totally unexpected complication. The general declared, "I am not going to Hanoi with you, but you go." He said, "I have too many awful memories of the horrors perpetrated on the South by the North. I also resent the North for killing American troops." I could see the agony on his face.

In the end, after much back-and-forth, Schwarzkopf agreed to accompany us, although he said fiercely, "I'll have nothing to do with any official in the North." I assured him he would not. I kept my word. Rather, the producers, and I went to dinner with some government officials in Hanoi while the general, clearly exhausted and troubled, remained at the hotel. He also stayed there while we filmed the city of Hanoi.

As I rode in the back of a rickshaw, Hanoi felt like a provincial French city of the 1960s with ancient districts and wards. There were very few of the high-rise buildings of the kind that had begun to dot the cityscape of Ho Chi Minh City in the South. I saw the now heavily polluted lake in the center of town where Navy aviator and future US senator John McCain was shot down on a bombing mission. It was now surrounded by low-rise buildings on three sides. How could it be so calm and peaceful? It felt hideous to visualize McCain and the other POWs in those waters. Visitors to the site were silent as they reverently remembered the atrocities that had happened there.

During the war there had been much talk about the conflict between free enterprise and communism. Coca-Cola, the symbol of free enterprise, was banned in North Vietnam. So, imagine our surprise when Rather, the general, and I checked into the International Hotel in Hanoi and found cans of Coke lining the inside of our refrigerators. Moreover, when I went down to the desk there were Vietnamese women dressed in *ao dai*, the native dress, a long tight-fitting tunic with sleeves worn over silk slacks. When some French tourists came to the desk and spoke French, the women behind the desk firmly replied, "We only speak English." It felt so odd. Vietnam had been under the control of France for decades. Clearly, those days were over.

Now, almost twenty years after the war ended, we could see that much of the ruined vegetation had grown back in this lush, tropical climate. There was little evidence of the battles that had been fought on that land. Americans were greeted warmly and graciously both in the North and the South. We were very surprised. Despite all the destruction and heartbreak the United States had suffered and inflicted in those fields, the scars of war seemed to have faded. Rather and the general were incredulous. "Who would have thought," they said almost in unison, "that this would be the result?"

Schwarzkopf also admitted another psychological conundrum. "I am a different man today about Vietnam because of the Gulf War. I don't know how to explain that except to say, I was crushed by the fact that the American people had rejected me and my profession for doing what our government told us to do."

During the Gulf War and after, that changed. He was revered as "a hero" and *People Magazine* called him a "grizzly bear of a man with a teddy bear side." All we saw on this trip was the teddy bear. He had his ideas and expressed them but never gave orders. Years later, I met an officer who had served with Schwarzkopf and remembered the violent temper that earned him the nickname "Stormin'Norman." I saw no evidence of that in his return visit to Vietnam.

At the end, the general admitted, "Coming to Hanoi was the toughest part of the trip. I expected the worst. I don't know what I expected to see, but Hanoi is just another city."

I returned to New York to edit the program and then flew down to Tampa to screen the finished product for the general. US Central Command (Centcom) is headquartered in Tampa, and Schwarzkopf had remained there after retiring from the military as Centcom commander. We watched the documentary *Schwarzkopf in Vietnam: A Soldier Returns* in his office. At the conclusion, the general turned to me and said, through tears, "The war's over but it really wasn't over for me until I went back."

# *17*

# TOO CLOSE TO CALL

The presidential election of 2000 was one of the darkest hours in the history of television news. Early on November 8, long before sunrise, the networks and the cable news channels declared that Republican governor George W. Bush of Texas would be the forty-third president of the United States, defeating his Democratic opponent, Vice President Al Gore. Two hours later, around 4:00 a.m. eastern time, they took it back.

The race had come down to Florida and its twenty-five electoral votes. The first signs of the disaster that was about to unfold came early on election night, November 7. Just before 8:00 p.m., the networks called Florida for Gore, but questions were soon raised about the accuracy of that call. And two hours later, around 10:00 p.m., they withdrew Florida from the Gore column and said the state was then considered too close to call.

At 2:00 a.m., the networks again called a winner in Florida, but this time it was Bush. And they declared him the next president. But as results from Florida continued to come in, Bush's lead there continued to shrink, until just a few hundred votes separated him from Gore. In an embarrassment of historic proportions, the networks retracted Florida— again—and with it, the presidential call. No one knew who the next president would be.

I remember newspaper headlines blaring: "A Flawed Call Leads to High Drama" (*NYT*); "Networks Try to Explain Blown Call" (AP); "Forecasting System Backfires on TV" (*Boston Globe*); and "Why Couldn't the Media Get It Right?" (*Miami Herald*).

For the past twenty-five years, I had had various election-night assignments, from the field to the studio. For the past ten years or so, I had been Correspondent Bruce Morton's producer on the analysis desk. Election nights were exciting, and you could feel the electricity in the studio as we scrambled to give meaning to the election results.

But in 2000, I had no election assignment. Like millions of Americans, I watched the Bush-Gore presidential election results on TV at home. When the night was over, neither candidate had the 270 votes needed to win the Electoral College. Gore received 48.4 percent of the popular vote while Bush received 47.9 percent.

For more than a month, the nation did not know who the next president would be. The recount of Florida ballots began and there were court battles. On December 12, just three days before the Electoral College was scheduled to meet, the US Supreme Court, in a 5–4 decision, ordered the vote count be stopped. The earlier certification of Bush as the winner in Florida (made by the Republican secretary of state) would stand. Bush would get Florida's electoral votes and the presidency, by a whisker. Bush had 271 electoral votes, one more than required. Gore got 266 electoral votes, though he won 547,398 more popular votes than Bush.

Some Republicans claimed that the networks had been biased in their early calls when they declared Democrat Gore the winner. This gave Congressman Billy Tauzin (R-LA) an opportunity to hold hearings before the Committee on Commerce, which he chaired. He wrote to the network presidents, "Our own analysis of the networks' election night 'victory calls' indicates an incontrovertible bias in the reports which were reported."

This was a very serious charge, and all the network presidents testified. CBS News president Heyward, Dr. Kathleen Frankovic (director of surveys at CBS News), one of the coauthors of the CBS report, and I went over the CBS report, line by line. Frankovic and I accompanied Heyward to Washington, where we waited outside the committee hearing room with the other network presidents for five hours while other election business was heard. The presidents were angry at waiting and at having to testify under oath on a subject that was, they claimed, a strictly journalistic matter. Roger Ailes, Fox chairman, said, "I am deeply disappointed that this is being handled as an investigative and not as a legislative fact-finding matter. I am further disappointed that this committee views its role as adversarial, requiring us to take an oath as if we have something to hide. We do not. With or without a swearing-in photo, we will hide nothing."

Louis D. Boccardi, president and chief executive officer of the Associated Press, said, "fixing them (the voting errors) is a job for the nation's editors, not its legislators."

The network presidents cited reports done by their organizations after the election, pinpointing the source of the errors. These were serious and never should have happened.

So how did they?

I was asked to head the CBS News investigation because I worked with standards, had not worked that election, and was a veteran of political reporting and election nights. I felt the challenge of this assignment, but how could I explain what had happened? What would my colleagues think? I might well have to cite them for some of the mistakes. Fortunately, I had help: Dr. Kathleen Frankovic and Dr. Kathleen Hall Jamieson, dean of the Annenberg School of Communication at the University of Pennsylvania. It took the three of us about six weeks to prepare our detailed, eighty-seven-page report.

We were all shocked at some of the procedures used to predict winners. ABC, CBS, CNN, Fox, NBC, and the Associated Press had set up a consortium, Voter News Service, VNS, to count the vote nationwide. VNS took partial blame for sharing erroneous data. It had grossly understated the number of voters in two key Florida counties. One reason: A keypunch operator entered the wrong numbers into the computer. Another problem was the so-called "butterfly ballots" in Palm Beach County. The layout, listing ten presidential candidates, was confusing. Some people who thought they were voting for Democrat Al Gore were voting for conservative Pat Buchanan, the Reform Party candidate. Then VNS admitted another mistake: "We did not correctly anticipate the impact of the absentee vote."

There was plenty of blame to go around. It wasn't just the incorrect VNS numbers but also what each news organization's decision desk did with them. Each network's decision desks took the VNS information and combined it with other data, unique to each network. The experts on each desk had charts of past races and lists of possible deviations. They weighed all the information, including the VNS vote count, before they declared the result. I knew that the CBS decision desk, to quote the CBS report, "Is the engine that drives the election night train." That desk works in tandem with the executive producer of the election broadcast and the president of CBS News to determine what goes on the air. But on election night 2000, CBS News correspondent Byron Pitts in Florida was reporting a first: Thousands of people were still waiting in line to vote several hours after the polls had closed. Anyone in CBS New York Studio 47 could hear that Florida, the key to the election, had not yet finished voting.

We could hear Rather and Pitts chatting on air that the outcome would probably be delayed due to all the voters waiting in line. Not a minute later there was a bulletin from VNS declaring Bush had won Florida, and all the networks went with the bulletin. It was normal in those days for all the networks to simply accept a decision as announced by VNS. In the CBS case, the decision desk was isolated from the newsroom and could not hear what the news team was saying about votes continuing in Florida. Perhaps if they had, CBS would not have made the call.

After our investigation, we recommended several major changes: The decision desk should be in the main broadcast studio so our analysts could hear what was happening in the field. The information about people waiting to vote should have raised serious caution in the Florida call. We also recommended that there be no call until all polls in a state were closed. (The first Florida call for Gore, by NBC, had come a few minutes before poll closing time in the state.) We recommended that a vice president head the desk to decide exactly when CBS had enough information to make this critical call. I was given that assignment in future elections.

I knew enough about the whole process to supervise, which is what I did for the next six national elections. After discussions with analysts on the decision desk, I was charged with saying "go" or "no go" for each call. As you can imagine, this sometimes led to heated discussions with the broadcast executive producer, the president of CBS News, and the anchor, Dan Rather. It was a huge challenge, but I slowly grew more confident.

We also changed our on-air terminology. We no longer "called" races or "declared" winners. We "estimated" them and "projected" them, making clear that these were not the final, official results, which come from government election officials only. We were also more transparent about the way we made estimates and projections, telling viewers they were based on polling of voters after they cast their ballots, returns from key districts, and the raw vote.

In addition, there was a thorough investigation of Voter News Service. CBS and the other VNS members brought in one of the top computer programming companies in the country to make sure the problems were fixed in time for the next election. While 2002 was a midterm election, all 435 House seats and one-third of the Senate seats would be decided. Despite the best efforts, the VNS situation only got worse. On election night, November 5, 2002, the VNS computers failed. This was the last straw!

All five networks and the AP agreed that shutting down VNS was the only way to go. To replace it, they formed the National Election Poll (NEP) to prepare a system for getting election information from the polls to the news organizations. NEP provided election-night exit polling. Across the country, as voters left polling places, they were asked to fill out a short anonymous questionnaire. From their answers, NEP could share the characteristics of the voters: men, women; poor, middle class, wealthy; education; liberal, conservative. NEP would also know for whom they voted. In a separate operation, AP collected the vote count from the secretary of state of each of the fifty states.

This system was finally ready for the presidential election of 2004, between President George W. Bush and his Democratic challenger, Senator John Kerry of Massachusetts. I was nervous as I stepped into my role as safety valve for CBS News. As the night wore on, the pressure was building for decisions. I received calls from the president of CBS News, "Linda, what are we waiting for?" I responded, "We just don't see it yet." And when another network called a state: "Linda," said a loud voice, "what are we waiting for?" "To have the correct analysis." I stuck to my guns. I had learned a great deal.

The combination newsroom-studio was extremely noisy. People were shouting out breaking developments even as Dan Rather was on the air. Teams in the studio reported the presidential, Senate, and House races. Since the decision desk was now in the studio, we could hear those reports coming in from the field and advise colleagues if something seemed wrong. The new system was working well. I respected our various election experts who used information from former elections and other statistical reports to share a sense of what was happening. One of our experts knew every precinct in America. "The pattern doesn't look correct," he would say. "This is a precinct of older voters and since it's raining, that population won't be able to get out to vote so early." I felt it was critical to have human gut input checking the computers and their algorithms. "Unless you all agree on the result, we will not announce it," I told our experts. I could hear the experts' discussions. "How did you account for a certain county in the last election?" asked one. "What do we know about those who have voted up until now?" another expert asked. "Is there some bloc waiting to vote that might sway the state's total as it did (two? four?) years ago?" It was necessary to listen to these extremely smart people gathering the information needed to convince each other of the outcome. Only when they agreed on which candidate was likely to win would I give the go-ahead for Rather to announce it on the air.

Election night 2004 was hardly a repeat of 2000, but it had its own drama. Florida, Pennsylvania, and Ohio became the key states to watch as the hours went by. All the networks called Pennsylvania for Kerry at 11:00 p.m., eastern time, and they called Florida for Bush by 12:24 a.m. Ohio was a problem, though. Our correspondent in the field kept talking about "provisional" votes and the crowds still in line to vote. I was getting calls from the president of CBS News, Heyward, and Rather, on edge, asking, "Why can't we call Ohio?" "Because our experts don't have enough data," I replied. Polls kept closing in other states and all the networks and cables were reporting the wins. Ohio remained the last big prize, and the 123,548 provisional ballots cast there would decide the presidency. Provisional ballots were given to voters at the polls for a variety of reasons: their name may not have appeared on the poll list, their signature may not have matched the signature on the registration form, or they may have lacked valid identification. Each ballot's eligibility had to be checked after the polls closed.

Aware that the provisional ballots had not yet been verified and counted, I insisted, "We cannot project Ohio." CBS and ABC held off, but NBC, Fox, and CNN gave Ohio to Bush, though they hedged their bets, not calling any other state after Ohio because that might have predicted the winner before anyone really knew for sure. When

Heyward told me NBC had called Ohio, I said "Fine. They're using the same information from NEP, but their decision models are interpreting it differently." I felt extraordinary pressure, but with the backing of the experts on the decision desk, I held my ground. "We're not calling Ohio." The numbers in the state were so close, the presidential election result was not announced until Kerry conceded to Bush the next day around noon. I continued to head the decision desk for the next four national elections. For sure, none of those elections was as dramatic as 2000 and 2004.

Four presidential elections later, in an election I did not cover, Republican Donald Trump upset the 2016 NEP predictions and won the Electoral College while losing the popular vote. It was the fifth time that had happened in US history. Democrat Hillary Clinton had been the favorite and the expected winner. However, there were warning signs early in the evening that she could lose. A little after 9:00 p.m., it was reported that a handful of states she was expected to win went instead for Trump. Just after eleven o'clock, Trump was projected as the forty-fifth president in a stunning upset. He had won the Electoral College, 304–227, even though Clinton won nearly three million more popular votes than Trump. She did not make her concession speech until the next morning.

# 18

## 9 / 11

It was a beautiful late summer morning that felt more like early fall. The sun was shining. The air was cool and crisp. I was getting ready to go to work when it happened. A little after 9:00 a.m., there was a report of an explosion at the World Trade Center (WTC) in Lower Manhattan. It was September 11, 2001. New York City would never be the same, and I found myself in the middle of the biggest story of the decade.

Details kept trickling in. The explosion was caused by a plane crashing into the North Tower of the WTC. Soon live television cameras were focused on the burning building as flames shot out the sides. Within minutes viewers watched in horror as a second plane hit the South Tower. It was clear now; this was no accident.

My husband, Cary, and my daughter, Beth, were glued to the TV set in our home just north of Manhattan. With the main highway into the city now closed, I was working on the computer, searching frantically for an alternative way to get to the office.

All these years later, Beth tells me she was extremely frightened when I finally jumped into the car heading toward the office. Cary, a former CBS reporter who reported from Vietnam amidst gunfire, knew it was part of my job and was less worried.

As I drove to the office, the images of the Twin Towers on fire replayed in my mind over and over. As I had done so many times as a producer, I was trying to turn those pictures into a story. I listened to the fragmented reports on the radio for any new details that would help me stitch it together and make sense of what had happened. We soon learned the two planes had been hijacked. And at 9:37 a.m. a third plane crashed into the Pentagon, just outside Washington. A fourth plane, also commandeered by the terrorists and believed to be heading to Washington, would crash into a field in Pennsylvania after a struggle between the hijackers and passengers forced it down by the passengers. At 10:00 a.m., the South Tower at the WTC collapsed; the North Tower collapsed half an hour later.

President George W. Bush was in Sarasota, Florida, visiting the Emma E. Booker Elementary School, where he was in a classroom reading with a group of young children. He had been told earlier that a plane had hit the North Tower. Then, as the president was reading a storybook with the class of young children, suddenly, White House chief of staff Andy Card leaned over and whispered in his ear. Years later, the president told a documentary producer, "Andy Card comes up behind me and says, 'Second plane has hit the second tower. America is under attack.' And I'm watching a child read." Bush recalled, "And then I see the press in the back of the room beginning to get the same message that I just got.

"And I could see that horror . . . on the faces of the news people who had just gotten the same news. During a crisis it's important to set a tone and not to panic," he continued. "And so, I waited for the appropriate moment to leave the classroom." At 9:30 a.m. President Bush announced to the world that the United States had been attacked. Nothing like this had ever happened before.

As I ran into the huge CBS newsroom, reporters were trying to figure out what had taken place. Several CBS News reporters and camera crews were already on scene in the smoke-filled area near the World Trade Center. Correspondent Harold Dow, there from the beginning, reported, "It is surreal and devastating . . . an unbelievable situation." Dow found shelter in a store belowground at the subway.

The newsroom was in shock. So were New Yorkers as they heard the news and watched the once blue sky turn gray as the smoke spread from downtown Manhattan. I attended a meeting to discuss what we knew and then set out to be the most helpful I could be—answering phones from people in the field and relaying that information to the production crew that was live-broadcasting the news. I was now a vice president so I could perform the range of tasks I had done on my way up: answer phones, dig up breaking news, help package it, and put my finger in the dike wherever help was needed. I shared facts with our reporters and suggested people to interview. I was also available to perform any task needed. I shared other information I learned as well.

Correspondents, cameramen, and sound technicians started returning to the newsroom in Midtown Manhattan covered with white ash and looking shell-shocked, a testament to what they had witnessed. We set up a place for them to clean up and rest with food and coffee before they went out again. This continued for days.

Dan Rather anchored our coverage for fourteen straight hours before finally passing the baton at 2:00 a.m. on September 12. He returned to the anchor desk later that morning as CBS News live television coverage continued around the clock for four straight days.

It was a very unsettling time for New York City residents, let alone the entire country and the world. In interviews, New Yorkers shared their questions and their fears. Was this the way of the future? The United States had never been attacked on the mainland. How safe were we going to be?

At 9:00 p.m., on that fateful Tuesday, President Bush addressed the nation from the Oval Office, declaring, "Terrorist attacks can shake the foundations of our biggest buildings, but they cannot touch the foundation of America. These acts shatter steel, but they cannot dent the steel of American resolve."

In the end, the nineteen hijackers were Islamic terrorists—mainly from Saudi Arabia and several other Arab nations. Reportedly financed by the al Qaeda terrorist organization of Saudi fugitive Osama bin Ladin, they were allegedly acting in retaliation for America's support of Israel, its involvement in the Persian Gulf War, and its continued military presence in the Middle East.

The attack had been planned for more than a year. Some of the terrorists had lived in the United States for longer and had taken flying lessons at American commercial flight schools. Others had slipped into the country in the months before September 11 to act as the "muscle" in the operations.

That night, when I left for home after 2:00 a.m., I had to search for an open bridge off the main road since the US government had closed all major bridges into New York City, and I lived across the Hudson River. Driving home I saw huge Mack trucks piled with wreckage being transported from the WTC site to dumps upstate. I continued to see this night after night as 1.8 billion tons of wreckage was removed from "the pile." It took more than six months to clean it all out.

Reporters from the scene that day summed up the situation: CBS reporter Carol Marin told Dan Rather, "I think I was in the second collapse or an explosion after that. I was coming toward the WTC looking for CBS crews and asked a firefighter if he saw any. He told me to walk down the middle of the road . . . Suddenly there was a roll, an explosion and we could see a ball of flame coming at us . . . He and others screamed '*Run*' and I fell. Someone picked me up. We ran as fast as we could, then he threw me into the wall of a building and covered me with his body . . . I was pretty sure we were going to die."

Smoke from the second tower began rushing toward CBS cameraman Mark LaGanga. People were sprinting by him, running for their lives. But LaGanga planted his feet and pointed his camera. "I knew the smoke was coming towards me," he said. "But the reason you don't turn, drop the camera, and run away is because you're there to document what happens."

As the smoke got closer, people were falling to the ground, forced down by the intensity of the smoke plume. Then it reached LaGanga and his camera. His lens was covered with residue from the explosion, but he never stopped filming. For three minutes and fourteen seconds, LaGanga recorded the sounds of coughing and sporadic yelling, all in total darkness. Then LaGanga began to dust off his camera and resume filming. Like LaGanga, reporters and technicians in the field just felt they were doing their job and needed no special recognition. That's one reason I'm using their names in this chapter.

Correspondent Scott Pelley was working to finish a *60 Minutes* report. When he heard the news, he immediately headed downtown. He tried to call CBS on his cell phone only to find the communications system had collapsed with the towers. He spotted a pay phone. With no change in his pocket, he picked up the phone just to see and indeed it was operational! The phone company had switched to emergency mode, activating all pay phones for coin-free calls. He phoned in his report.

Pelley worked downtown for the next few days and created a system to get his reports back to CBS headquarters. Pelley remembers, "A producer came down with a wad of hundred-dollar bills and we would shoot a story about what was happening at Ground Zero, flag down a random passing car, give the driver a hundred-dollar bill and ask that the tape be delivered to CBS headquarters. And then we'd move on to the next report."

For weeks, New Yorkers lined the roads near the WTC ruins and firehouses applauding the firefighters and police officers who saved lives that day and were now helping to restore order and searching for the missing. It was so sad to see photos of the missing on light poles and trees, hung there by loved ones hoping to learn their fate. Only twenty survivors were plucked from the rubble where more than 2,500 died. The fire continued to burn for three months.

On Thanksgiving 2001, Elissa was home from college and I took my family to view the ruins from an observation deck on the roof of a tall building several blocks away. The press had set up this vantage point overlooking the entire scene, sixteen acres of ruin. Thinking of the more than 2,500 people who lay among those ruins was almost too much to grasp.

A monument built to honor the dead opened on September 11, 2010. It is one of the top ten tourist attractions in New York City. I have seen aerial photos of the sixteen-acre site. It seems peaceful with trees and two pools, each an acre in size, with the names of all who died that day carved into the rims. For me, the aerial view is as close to the monument as I care to get.

# 19

# CRISIS SHAKES CBS NEWS
# TO ITS ROOTS

In the fall of 2004, with the United States deeply entangled in wars in Iraq and Afghanistan, President George W. Bush was locked in a tight race for reelection against his Democratic challenger, Massachusetts senator and Vietnam War hero John Kerry. Less than eight weeks before Election Day, CBS aired an exclusive and explosive report that could well have ended Bush's hopes for a second term. Instead, it cost some top CBS journalists their jobs and nearly destroyed CBS News.

The report alleged that in the late 1960s, at the height of the Vietnam War, Bush used his father's influence to get a plumb position as a pilot in the Texas Air National Guard (TANG).

That assignment would have probably kept him from fighting in Vietnam. The report charged that Bush failed to meet his service requirements. These charges had been floated for years, but in this new report Dan Rather and Producer Mary Mapes declared they had found *the authentic* documents—just discovered—proving the charges. There was just one problem for CBS: The report, it turned out, was based on documents that could not be verified.

An independent review panel commissioned by CBS News came to that conclusion after a three-month investigation. The panel also stated that the source of the documents, retired Texas Army National Guard Lt. Col. Bill Burkett, was a controversial figure and unreliable. Mapes told the panel, "She was aware of the news reports at the time about Burkett, but she was not involved in any of the contemporaneous reporting related to Lt. Col. Burkett given she was then investigating the Abu Ghraib Iraq prison scandal. The panel views the plea of ignorance of this news coverage as significant because . . . such information could have been accessed through Internet or Lexis-Nexis searches."

The story aired two days after Labor Day, on the program *60 Minutes Wednesday*. The CBS report and the supporting documents were immediately called into question by the White House and GOP leaders. For nearly two weeks, CBS News defended the report, until it was finally determined that the documents were, probably, fake. Dan Rather, who had broken the story, was forced to make an embarrassing on-air apology.

How could this have happened?

Rather and his producer, Mary Mapes, were a highly regarded, award-winning team—considered among the best in the business. Earlier in the year, they had revealed, with graphic photos, how American soldiers abused Iraqi inmates at the Abu Ghraib prison near Baghdad. That report, which aired on *60 Minutes II*, earned them a prestigious George Foster Peabody award. It also earned them even greater confidence from their colleagues that their reporting could be trusted.

Rather and Mapes had received tips questioning Bush's military service as far back as the presidential campaign of 2000, when Bush defeated former vice president Al Gore. The tips did not lead to a story then; but in 2003, the team began following new tips. In late August and early September of 2004, Mapes was reporting the story largely on her own because Rather was tied up with other responsibilities, including covering the Republican National Convention in New York City, at which Bush was renominated, and then Hurricane Frances, which struck Florida Labor Day weekend.

On the Friday before the holiday, Mapes received two memos from Bill Burkett. The next day, he shared four more memos. Mapes believed she now had the evidence to prove the case that Bush had failed to meet his military obligations. She told Josh Howard, the executive producer of *60 Minutes*, the weekday edition, that she'd have the report ready for Wednesday's broadcast, just four days away.

But before the report could air, the authenticity of the typewritten memos had to be verified. And that is where the trouble began. Mapes and her reporting team had virtually no experience authenticating documents. Document documentation was not something producers dealt with on a day-to-day basis, and Mapes admitted she knew little about the skill, joking in her book, "at that point, you could have put everything I knew about document analysis on the head of a pin and still had room for the state of Texas."

The memos were photocopies. The team did not know that only originals can be verified because the ink and the paper need to be tested. Mapes hired four handwriting experts. But they were only capable of verifying signatures, not the documents themselves. Of the six documents, only one had a full signature—Lt. Col. Jerry Killian—Bush's commanding officer. Two had only initials and three had no handwriting at all. Two of the handwriting experts said the signature might be genuine, while the two others had doubts. The doubters were dismissed. And on Wednesday, September 8, the report aired on CBS.

Within minutes, the authenticity of the memos was questioned by the mostly conservative websites freerepublic.com, Powerlineblog.com, and littlegreenfootballs.com. And by the next afternoon, the powerful Drudge Report website had joined the fray. CBS News was deluged with calls, letters, and Web comments. It was a perfect storm for the bloggers to call out the mainstream media in a major way. It was a watershed moment—one of the first instances in which the Web challenged a network news report—and succeeded.

CBS News was under siege. Even as CBS was defending the report publicly, President Andrew Heyward asked me how we could best investigate potential flaws in the reporting. I suggested we convene an outside panel because, I argued, "if we only have CBS people examine the situation, it might be called a cover-up." Heyward agreed.

Less than two weeks after the report aired, CBS News acknowledged the documents could not be verified. For one thing, when showing the documents to the Texas Air National Guard, it was determined they were not formatted to the TANG style, but to that of the Texas Army National Guard, a separate division of the Texas military. On September 18, Burkett admitted in an on-camera interview with Rather that he deliberately misled the CBS producer working on the report, giving her a false account of the documents' origins to protect a promise of confidentiality to the actual source. CBS News president Andrew Heyward went public and said, "Based on what we now know, CBS News cannot prove that the documents are authentic, which is the only acceptable journalistic standard to justify using them in the report . . . that was a mistake, which we deeply regret."

Rather stated, "If I knew then what I know now—I would not have gone ahead with the story as it was aired, and I certainly would not have used the documents in question." Rather later told the Thornburgh panel investigating the incident that "he did not fully agree with this decision and still believes that the content of the documents is accurate." The panel was troubled by these conflicting statements, but the fact remained that the documents could not be verified.

After the apologies, CBS News announced two days later that an outside panel would investigate the report. This was done with the approval of CBS chairman and CEO Leslie Moonves, who had promised a public investigation. It would be conducted by respected journalist Louis D. Boccardi, who had retired the previous year as president and CEO of the Associated Press, and Republican Richard Thornburgh, who had served as US Attorney General under presidents Ronald Reagan and George H. W. Bush.

Thornburgh was chosen to head the panel. I later explained that decision in a deposition for the panel, "CBS News is known as a somewhat liberal organization and we felt someone who didn't come with a liberal bias would be able to deliver a report that would be accepted both within CBS News and the world at large." Heyward said in his deposition, "Choosing one Republican member for the panel worked brilliantly because the panel found there was no political bias in the (Bush) report, a very positive conclusion for CBS News and for Mr. Rather's reputation." (Rather had objected to the selection of Thornburgh because of his ties to George W. Bush's father.)

Heyward could not be a part of the investigative process, since he had screened the report before it aired. He instructed me, "Work with the panel to get them any information and video they might need and be the liaison with Les Moonves (the CBS chairman) since the corporation is very much involved." During all my years at CBS News, I'd had very few dealings with the corporation. It was an unwritten understanding that the corporation would not interfere with the reporting of CBS News.

As the investigation proceeded, colleagues continually badgered me. "Why are lawyers on the panel?" I was direct, "Lawyers are finders of facts presented to a jury." I pointed out, there is also a journalist, Lou Boccardi, on the panel. Beyond that, I was not allowed to reveal anything about the panel's work. For months, I felt as if I were in isolation, quarantined. It was a very difficult time for me since I was used to being involved in all the events CBS was covering and talking with my colleagues.

I was in touch with panel members daily to answer their questions, not specifically about the Bush report but how CBS News operates. "How does CBS News ensure reporting is accurate? What is needed to determine if a document is genuine?" My role was to explain our reporting methods, not to sway the panel in any way. I said we wanted them to work independently. We did not want to appease anyone, we wanted to find the truth.

Meanwhile, Mapes was anxious to prove her story, but she had been ordered to stop reporting. She came to me, very upset. I was sympathetic and thought her follow-up suggestions made sense, so I asked Heyward if we could hire a detective to pursue her leads. He agreed, but the detective's attempt to authenticate the memos failed. And after the two handwriting experts dismissed by Mapes told ABC News about their doubts, the clerk typist who worked with Lt. Col. Killian for years and was supposed to have created the original documents, Marian Carr Knox, told the *Dallas Morning News* she had never typed the memos and confirmed they were not written in the TANG format.

The Thornburgh panel spent three months interviewing more than sixty people and reviewing transcripts, e-mails, military records, and other documents. On Wednesday, January 5, 2005, seventeen weeks after the *60 Minutes* broadcast aired, the panel delivered its confidential findings to CBS News and the CBS corporation. Four days later, on Sunday, Moonves convened a meeting at his office in Black Rock, the granite skyscraper in Midtown Manhattan that served as CBS corporate headquarters. Moonves had read the full 224-page report. And now he gathered News president Heyward, me, CBS lawyers, and members of the CBS press office to discuss what to do about it. The next day, CBS made the report public.

It was devastating.

The panel blamed "A rush to air the reports which overwhelmed the proper application of CBS News Standards." The report laid out a "litany of missteps" and "failures." It said efforts to authenticate the documents that were the basis of the Bush report "failed miserably." "Only the most cursory effort" was made to establish the chain of custody of the documents. "Valid questions" that were raised about the report before air were "pushed aside instead of probed." Given Mapes's "reputation and stature," the panel said, the vetters did not press her for the answers they needed before approving the report.

As I read the Thornburgh report, I felt CBS News had been betrayed by the Rather-Mapes team. It was a case of jumping to conclusions without the facts. Facts, then conclusions are a basic tenet of journalism. The incident blackened the reputations of the proud journalists who worked at CBS News.

On the day the report was released, Thornburgh told the *PBS NewsHour*, "If you're looking for a villain in this case, we have one. It is *haste*. The haste with which this program was put together cut short the necessary vetting to authenticate the whole process."

The source of the documents, Bill Burkett, was well-known as a whistleblower, yet Mapes took him at his word even knowing that whistleblowers are not always reliable. She never tried to check his reputation with other CBS News Washington reporters who questioned Burkett's reliability. That reliability had been questioned in a February 12, 2004, *CBS Evening News* report. To confirm his authenticity would have delayed airing the report. Only later did Mapes learn Burkett was known as a "Bush-hater and unreliable source." In an on-camera interview with Rather, two weeks after the September 8 broadcast, Burkett confessed he had "misled" CBS News.

Mapes admitted she did not have time to do all the checking that was needed before the September 8 broadcast. She claimed she wanted to delay the report, but that Executive Producer Josh Howard insisted it air on the eighth. Howard disputes this, saying he had another story that could have aired in its place.

In her 2005 book, Mapes continued to defend that the memos were the real deal, stating, "I came to a well-grounded conclusion that these documents appeared to be true in every way," and "The overwhelming evidence in any impartial appraisal of the Killian memos, based on both content and form, is that they are authentic."

The panel cited another critical error. Executive Producer Howard told Mapes she could not serve as an intermediary to put the source (Burkett) in contact with the Kerry campaign. But the panel reports Mapes told them, "She was seeking to use the Kerry campaign . . . as a means of persuading Lt. Col. Burkett to provide additional documents for her report." He had requested this contact as his price for handing over the documents. The panel called this "a clear conflict of interest in that it created the appearance of a political bias." It also violated CBS News standards.

The fallout from the panel's report came quickly.

Mary Mapes was fired outright, and it was the beginning of the end of Dan Rather's storied career at CBS. In March of 2005, he left the *CBS Evening News* anchor chair. It was later learned that in the months before the Bush report aired, Rather had been negotiating to step down the following year, in March of 2006, upon his twenty-fifth anniversary as anchor and managing editor. Rather spent his final year at CBS News on the original *60 Minutes*. He left CBS in June 2006, after forty-four years at the network.

The very talented team of Senior Vice President Betsy West, Executive Producer Josh Howard, and Senior Producer Mary Murphy, all involved with the Bush report, were asked to resign. Another senior producer was demoted.

In November of 2005, News president Andrew Heyward left CBS, a delayed casualty of the Bush memo crisis. Senior Vice President Marcy McGuinness was also asked to leave. She had nothing to do with the Bush report, but new management wanted a fresh start. Of the 2004 CBS News editorial management team, only I remained.

Sean McManus, president of CBS Sports, was named president of CBS News and Sports. Thankfully, it was easy for me to help McManus acclimate to CBS News because he was a self-proclaimed news "junkie." Together, McManus and I ran the news division. Six months later, McManus hired Paul Friedman as vice president of "hard" or breaking news. Friedman had had long careers at NBC and ABC.

In the fall of 2007, just when we all thought the horrible incident was finally over, Dan Rather, no longer at CBS, sued CBS for seventy million dollars in New York State Supreme Court. He claimed his reputation had been ruined, that he was unable to search for another job, and that he had not gotten the amount of airtime he was promised for his last year at *60 Minutes*. He said if he won the lawsuit, he'd give the money to investigative reporting and other worthy news projects. The lawsuit was dismissed by a five-judge panel in September 2009. With that dismissal the ordeal was finally closed, five years after the controversial report had aired.

One of the recommendations of the Thornburgh panel was that CBS appoint a standards executive to make sure all investigative and controversial reports be checked once while they are in progress and again before they aired. Moonves called me into his office and said, "Linda, going forward you are the perfect person to take on that responsibility." I had never expected this. "Les, thank you for your confidence in me." "You deserve it," he said. "You helped me save CBS News. You'll now have the title of senior vice president." I marveled; in almost forty years I had climbed the ladder from the basement to the top rung at CBS News. I knew my already full plate had gotten fuller. And I knew how critical this new responsibility would be.

# 20

# HEARTACHE IN BAGHDAD

It was a phone call I will never forget. The CBS News desk awakened me at 5:00 a.m. on Memorial Day 2006 with the horrifying news that a car bomb in Iraq had killed two members of a CBS crew, Cameraman Paul Douglas and Soundman James Brolan. A third member, Correspondent Kimberly Dozier, thirty-nine years old, was "hanging on to life by a thread."

I immediately called Sean McManus, who had been president of CBS News for only six months. He, too, was shocked. We decided to leave immediately for Germany, where Dozier would be transported to be treated at the US Army's Landstuhl Regional Medical Center, the largest American military hospital outside the United States. On the way, we would stop in London to attend a memorial service for the men we lost. Douglas, age forty-eight, had worked for CBS for nearly seventeen years and was a popular member of the London bureau. He left a wife, two daughters, and three grandchildren. Brolan, age forty-two, had worked for CBS a little more than a year. He left a wife, son, and daughter.

As Kimberly Dozier writes in her book, *Breathing the Fire*, she was preparing a report on a US Army foot patrol on Memorial Day, revisiting the site where an Iraqi convoy had been hit the day before. The CBS team had come to see if there was more information that witnesses could share about what had happened. Suddenly, a battered Iraqi taxi, carefully packed with some five hundred pounds of explosives, exploded. Someone was watching and waiting for the right moment to trigger the explosion. The taxi was parked on a street used by Iraqi patrols. The American military patrol followed by an American network TV crew walked straight into what's called "the kill zone" of the ambush. Dozier notes, "the killers probably could not believe their luck." Now CBS had to pick up the pieces.

My husband drove me to JFK Airport, where I barely made the holiday evening flight to London. As I traveled, I was not only grieving our colleagues, but I was also wracked with nerves. In what condition would Kimberly be in? Would she be alive? And if so, would I be able to do anything to help her? McManus took a separate flight and met me in London. We joined the entire CBS News bureau at the deeply poignant service for Paul and James. Colleagues spoke about their commitment to often dangerous work, sharing some of Paul and James's accomplishments as their families sobbed. The circumstances were impossible to absorb. The anguish of grief was palpable.

After the service, McManus stayed behind in London to comfort the emotionally shattered staff at the bureau while I flew on to Frankfurt. From there, it was an hour's drive to Landstuhl, site of the incredible US military hospital for US service personnel wounded abroad. I checked in at the Ramstein Inn, a small hotel on the hospital grounds. The next morning, I went across the street to Fisher House, where the US government provided free housing for relatives of the wounded. Dozier's elderly parents had just arrived and were checking in. When I heard their names, I introduced myself. I could see the fright on their faces and the sadness in their eyes and it shook me. Kimberly later told me, "Dad had served with the Marines in the Pacific and was wounded at Iwo Jima during World War II. Mom had been a 'Rosie the Riveter' (the name given to women who worked in government factories making everything from bullets to airplanes for the war effort). Mom also raised the six of us children."

At the hospital, Dozier's parents, other family members, and I were escorted to a waiting room near her private ICU. Her boyfriend, Pete, had arrived earlier from New Zealand and was with her. The neurosurgeon talked frankly to the family, saying "Kimberly died several times but was brought back to life at a field hospital immediately after the blast. Her wounds were so severe, she needed to be taken to a better equipped field hospital, where surgeons removed shrapnel from her head. She also required a massive blood transfusion and continues to have transfusions daily." Then he added, "Her legs were severely wounded. She may have to lose one or both." However, the doctor also said, "Kimberly has passed the worst and now we have to see how far she can recover." It was a theme repeated often in the next few months: great hope coupled with painful treatments.

After her parents and family visited Kim in the ICU, it was my turn. I didn't know what to expect. When I saw Kim, she was virtually unconscious. Her shaved head had a huge red scar bearing witness to what she had endured. All the tubes, bandages, and beeping machines made me feel faint. I stayed only a few minutes and returned to the hotel.

Sean arrived late the second night. I met him at the car. "Is it too late to visit Kim's parents?" he asked. "We can try." We went to Fisher House and asked the front desk to call them. Although it was 10:00 p.m., Dozier's parents welcomed Sean, thanking him for coming and for the care their daughter was receiving. "In this short time," her father told Sean, "we have already seen improvement in Kim's condition, and we are optimistic."

Now it was time for Sean and me to visit Dozier together. It was just after midnight, but Landstuhl had no formal visiting hours. We would be able to see Dozier if she were still awake. We put on yellow paper robes and purple gloves to protect Dozier from our germs and then quietly entered her room. Indeed, she was awake, but hooked up to tubes and monitoring machines. It was awful. Not wanting to disturb her, we kept our visit short. Ironically, Dozier, who had just missed meeting Sean in New York on her way back to Baghdad, quipped, "Hey, Sean, next time I'd rather just meet for that drink, ok?" "It's a deal," Sean replied. How extraordinary! She still had her sense of humor. We smiled at her but, noticing her fatigue, I told her, "I'll be back tomorrow, Kim." Sean and I agreed we had witnessed a miracle.

It was well after midnight when we went to meet the CBS correspondents and crew who had come to Landstuhl to report the aftermath of the bombing. Correspondent Elizabeth Palmer would head on to Baghdad to cover events there. Correspondent Sheila MacVicar stayed in Germany and focused on Kim's recovery. And Charlie D'Agata reported the story for the CBS News syndication service. After that 3:00 a.m. meeting, Sean left Landstuhl for Frankfurt and the trip back to New York. I returned to the hotel.

Dozier stayed in the Landstuhl hospital only a week, but it seemed like forever. She appeared to be improving. She began sharing her memories, which the doctors found encouraging. "This is good news. We have been watching for signs of possible brain damage." But I also witnessed her constant pain when the bandages on her legs were removed and then replaced. She was anesthetized daily to undergo this procedure, and the doctors cited it as an "operation." In the weeks ahead, Kim endured more than forty operations of all kinds. Although all the blood in her body had been replaced, her resilience was extraordinary. And the doctors were able to save her legs.

Since my arrival in Germany, I had been talking with television and newspaper reporters from around the world. All were totally sympathetic. "May we report Kimberly's health status?" Having talked with Kim, I said, "Yes," and then I shared her news. This was a worldwide news story, not just Kim's and CBS's private tragedy. Kim agreed to several interviews with MacVicar, and CBS shared portions of them with other news outlets.

Fortunately, the medical care at Landstuhl is the best in the world for the most serious wounds of war. The doctors had all too much experience treating American service members flown in from Iraq and Afghanistan. Talking with the doctors, it became apparent how demanding their jobs were. They shared stories of the horrors they had seen. As I walked around the hospital grounds, I saw the newly wounded being transported into the hospital, one busload after another. It was shocking. CBS cameramen captured the images and shared them with the worldwide audience. I had never witnessed anything like this, made that much more poignant by our severely wounded colleague.

On the day before Kimberly was to leave Landstuhl for the United States, her boyfriend, Pete, came to me with a request. "Kim has asked about a sleeping bag that would help insulate her on the chilly military flight. As a war correspondent, she's traveled on army transport planes and knows they are drafty and cold." "Of course," I answered, and I asked a driver to take me into the tiny town of Landstuhl to see if we could find a Therm-a-Rest sleeping bag. After checking several stores, we found one! "It was a lifesaver," Kimberly later told me.

It was hard to believe that it was just a little over a week since Dozier was wounded. Now she was flying back to the States with Pete and a medical team to continue her treatment at Bethesda Naval Hospital in her home state of Maryland. She spent time there and then transferred to Kernan Rehabilitation Hospital, also in Maryland. She was discharged August 2, two months after the Baghdad attack, with her sense of humor intact. She put out a statement saying, "I am leaving hospitals behind, ahead of deadline . . . I've had a couple of setbacks and still face some minor surgery . . . I'm up on crutches and can even manage with a cane. It's not pretty, but I'm walking on my own."

My personal inspiration during those dark days was Kimberly herself. She never shrank from the tough tasks she faced on the road to recovery. And even as we were doing all we could to help her, she was setting an example for us on how to meet a difficult challenge.

As I traveled home from Germany, I reviewed my week. I was grateful that my years of work as a producer in the field had prepared me for the quick decisions I had to make—for Dozier and for CBS News—in a time of crisis. Producers often deal with the unexpected and must quickly and calmly find an alternative way to proceed. Each situation is different, but the key always is to remain cool under pressure. With each experience over the years, I grew more comfortable and confident. At Landstuhl, in a situation so grave it was truly "life or death," I followed a pattern that had served me well—weighing advice from those around me (in this case, Dozier's family and the medical staff)—before making decisions.

In those terrible early days after the attack, CBS did all we could so that Dozier was given the care she needed and Paul and James the honor they deserved.

# 21

## CRONKITE'S MEMORIAL SERVICE

It had been thirty-eight years since Walter Cronkite welcomed me to the *CBS Evening News* as the first woman producer on the broadcast. Now, it was time to say farewell to him. And I found myself in a familiar role: Walter Cronkite's producer, one last time.

Cronkite died July 17, 2009, at the age of ninety-two, after an illustrious and unparalleled career in journalism. CBS was ready to give him a memorial service befitting the institution he was. It would be big. For the venue, we chose Lincoln Center's Avery Fisher Hall, with a seating capacity of more than 2,700. I gathered a group to help me plan the service. We met with representatives of Lincoln Center at the office of CBS corporation chairman and CEO Leslie Moonves. When Moonves's reps made suggestions, I listened attentively. I knew well that there is no such thing as too much advice from people who know the boss and want to help another colleague.

Among the many decisions we had to make were what music would be played and when and who would speak and in what order. To pay tribute to the most trusted man in America, we invited the most powerful man in the world, President Barack Obama. He graciously agreed to speak, as did former president Bill Clinton.

The memorial was set for September 9. The week before the ceremony, Secret Service agents inspected the building, ensuring it was safe and secure for Obama and Clinton. Agents searched every corner of the concert hall and the surrounding areas. They even inspected the stage lights hanging from the ceiling to see if they could hide a sniper.

The Secret Service provided the lectern so there was no chance explosives could be planted inside. All the speakers used it; the presidential seal was added just before President Obama spoke.

Agents rode the elevators and suggested a safe route for the two presidents to follow to the hall. They counted the number of steps from the holding room where the presidents and members of the Cronkite family would stay before the ceremony. Clinton, who was age sixty-three at the time, had had quadruple heart surgery five years earlier and had difficulty climbing a long flight of stairs, so the agents mapped the shortest route.

I had no idea of the time necessary to prepare for a presidential visit. The day of the ceremony, agents cleared the airport for the arriving president, coordinated the motorcade to Manhattan, and did a security sweep of the hall before the audience was allowed inside.

On the Friday before the Monday memorial, my team was deep into final preparations. We met with Moonves and his staff in the impressive CBS corporate conference room. Twenty people sat around a huge table, including corporate vice presidents in charge of publicity and the people who had put together the Walter Cronkite tribute video that would be shown in the hall. I led the group through our plan. "At times like this, the president speaks last," I told Moonves, information I received from a Washington correspondent in response to my questions about presidential protocol. Speakers, including the president, would walk on to the stage unannounced when it was their turn to offer a tribute. Moonves was among the speakers. "Where will I enter and leave the podium?" he asked. I was ready with the answer because a Moonves associate had briefed me on questions our CEO might ask.

When I walked into Avery Fisher Hall the morning of the memorial, I could feel the anticipation of the thousands lining up for the service. Although it had been three decades since Walter was a nightly fixture in America's living rooms, people still felt deeply connected to him. He had bound the nation together during major national events, the grave and the glorious. In the audience were his CBS colleagues and a Who's Who of the television news business, including network anchors and news executives, past and present.

All participants in the memorial wore special passes to walk around the building. I chaperoned the Cronkite family: his son, Chip, and two daughters, Kathy and Nancy, whom I had met a few times over the years. I had also known his much beloved wife, Betsy, who had died four years before, after a sixty-five-year marriage. Presidents Obama and Clinton arrived with their Secret Service details and were introduced to the Cronkite family in the holding room. We then seated the Cronkites in the first row of the hall. On stage, the US Marine band, known as the president's band, played "Stars and Stripes Forever."

Sean McManus, president of CBS News and Sports, was the first of sixteen speakers. He told the audience Cronkite's "stature and influence will never be duplicated. Walter stood for integrity, perspective, professionalism, and a sense of humor."

Moonves, representing the CBS corporation, shared that when he was growing up, "Walter was there every evening to carry my family through all the stories that changed our world."

Singer Jimmy Buffett told stories of the years he spent at Cape Cod and Martha's Vineyard on Walter's two-masted yacht, *Wyntje*, named after a seventeenth-century Cronkite ancestor. Buffett talked of the hours spent at the helm with Captain Cronkite, who loved sailing and the sea. Buffett sang "Son of a Sailor Man" as we smiled and were moved as well.

Then Buzz Aldrin—the second man to walk on the moon—stood at the lectern. Aldrin credited Walter for spurring public enthusiasm for space and science. He remembered Walter laughing at himself after that first moon landing in 1969 because after all those years reporting on space, Cronkite admitted the momentous event left him "almost speechless. It turned out I didn't have anything to say at all except 'Man on the moon, oh boy, oh boy.'"

Andy Rooney of *60 Minutes* was one of Cronkite's closest and oldest friends. They had met as young reporters covering World War II, Cronkite for the *United Press* and Rooney for *Stars and Stripes*. Rooney narrated a video tribute to their sixty-year friendship.

Mickey Hart of the Grateful Dead was next, talking about Walter's great love of drums. In fact, Hart shared that toward the end of Walter's life, he learned to play the drums and played them once or twice a day. Who knew? Then Hart played one of Walter's favorite drum compositions.

Bob Schieffer, CBS News chief Washington correspondent and anchor of *Face the Nation*, spoke of the Cronkite he knew. "Walter

Cronkite off camera was the same as Walter Cronkite on camera . . . Walter was the most curious man I have ever met . . . and he wanted to know as much as he could about everything."

Then Wynton Marsalis and his jazz sextet took the floor. They paraded around the hall, through the aisles, playing New Orleans–style funeral jazz, bringing the audience to our feet, clapping along and swaying to the music. It was marvelous.

Nick Clooney, actor George Clooney's father, a newsman and close friend of the Cronkites, shared this remembrance, "My wife and I took Walter out to dinner several months before his death when Walter wasn't going out much anymore. Walter had his back to the restaurant, and no one had noticed him. But when Walter stood to leave, there was a visible intake of breath and then one by one the customers all stood up, did not say anything, did not applaud, because that is what you do when a gentleman is leaving the room."

President Obama offered the final tribute to "the man who chronicled our time." The president said, "I did not know Mr. Cronkite personally, but through all the events that came to define the twentieth century, Walter Cronkite was there, telling the story of the American Age . . . we are grateful to him . . . for illuminating our time and the opportunity he gave us to say, yes, we too were there." All of us were moved, tearful for our loss and thankful for all Walter gave us.

I received hundreds of letters and e-mails of gratitude and praise from people in the hall that day. I especially valued a note from Cronkite's daughter Nancy, who wrote, "I loved how personal it was and how so much of Dad's just plain niceness came through."

Throughout the memorial, a huge photograph hung over the stage. It was Walter, looking out at the audience, a big smile on his face, as if to say, "I am here to celebrate my life with you." And that is what we did—celebrate his extraordinary life. And if he was, indeed, looking down at us, I am sure he was pleased.

# 22

# THE FUTURE

## Digital News

Look around. Printed newspapers are disappearing, shut down by competition from the Web. Since early 2000, 20 percent fewer newspapers are being printed in the United States, affecting thousands of local communities. But some local newspapers have been growing, taking advantage of the digital progress and delivering newspapers on the Web. And publishers are finding digital delivery can be profitable. In fact, the *New York Times* reported that in the second quarter of 2020, the *Times* online income from advertising and subscriptions surpassed print income for the first time. Looking toward the future—no more *paper* in news*papers*.

Digital journalism changed the news forever on Memorial Day 2020, when a seventeen-year-old high school student, Darnella Frazier, used her cell phone to record the nine minutes and twenty-nine seconds of a Minneapolis police officer pressing his knee against the neck of a Black man named George Floyd, killing him. Floyd was being arrested for allegedly using a counterfeit twenty-dollar bill to pay for a pack of cigarettes.

That video flashed around the world and became the key piece of evidence leading to the conviction of Police Officer Derek Chauvin for murder. The three officers working with him were also found guilty. That recording was unique, no stopping and starting, just one continuous run. If the tape had stopped and started, questions could have been raised about what really happened if there were any pauses in the tape. But there were none. The tape showed the entire incident from start to finish. Frazier received a citation from the prestigious Pulitzer Prize committee, noting, "her video highlighted the crucial role of citizen journalism in the quest for truth and justice."

The Founding Fathers felt independent news reporting was essential for a democracy to survive. In fact, Benjamin Franklin felt strongly that citizens in a democracy needed to keep up with local news events so government could function properly. He led the move to include the establishment of post offices in Article 1, Section 8 of the Constitution, so local newspapers could be delivered to rural constituents.

On New Year's Day 2022, Jim VandeHei, CEO of Axios, a very successful Web news delivery system, announced that Axios would expand into local news. Axios promised to bring high-quality reporting by news teams to explain the economic, social, and political changes in each community it serves.

Eight months later, Axios signed a deal to sell the company to Cox Enterprises, Inc. The Axios management team will be on the board of Cox. Cox chairman Alex Taylor said, "A big part of this investment is to expand the number of local markets we serve. Local watchdog journalism is so important to the health of any community, and no one is more focused on building that out nationally than Axios."

And there have been other efforts to guarantee local news. In 2009, a group of journalists challenged the trend of dying local newspapers by forming the Institute of Non-Profit News (INN). The original twenty-seven nonprofit, nonpartisan member news-gathering organizations mushroomed to four hundred members in 2022 and continues to grow. These independent news operations are run as 501(c)(3) nonprofits and are funded by foundations and independent donors.

Reporters focus on local news from neighborhoods to large metropolitan areas. Some cover specific beats such as education, the environment, and health care. Their reports have exposed corruption, inspired legal and policy reforms, and alerted the public to environmental perils, financial scams, and faulty products. The reporters also inform communities about business and government issues that affect daily life. Nearly four thousand newspapers and TV stations across the country bought individual stories these reporters uncovered, earning the INN stations revenues to operate while sharing their important work with the rest of the country. Newspapers, without paper, but on a digital delivery system, will continue to survive and grow in numbers.

On another front, digital technology is providing investigative journalists with new tools for getting to the truth. They analyze raw data from a variety of sources, including time-stamped satellite photos and Facebook updates, to check and challenge the accuracy of stories circulating around the world. This "open-source reporting" has helped journalists identify white nationalists who assaulted counter-protesters during the August 2017 white supremacist rally in Charlottesville, Virginia. They also monitored the protests and riots in Ferguson, Missouri, following the fatal shooting of a Black man by a white police officer.

Surveying the current journalism scene, Carl Bernstein, who with Bob Woodward broke the Watergate story and is author of a new memoir recounting his early days as a journalist, is very critical of today's local news reporting. He told Anderson Cooper on CNN that, "Local newspapers are gone . . . If you look at local news on television, it's pretty much in disgrace all over America." He continues, "Local reporters shove a microphone in somebody's face, get a good quote that seems to be controversial, run back and put it on air."

Bernstein continues, "That's not the best obtainable version of the truth. It's trying to manufacture controversy. That's not what our job ought to be." Bernstein goes on to comment, "Today we see how much reporting—if it's called that—is done from people looking up things on Google and thinking, oh, that's how I am going to get the story . . . just report what Google says."

With all the sources of news online today, there is a profession dedicated to collecting Web articles, characterizing them, and making them easily available. These providers, called "news curators," make daily selections of stories to share. Their websites have become very popular, although some journalists accuse them of abandoning impartiality by presenting a point of view. Some would argue that journalism was never totally impartial, but surely opinion journalism is far more common today than it was in my day.

The technology of journalism has progressed to a whole new state since I wrote my first newspaper story for the *Middletown Record* in 1959. I used a clunky manual typewriter with a messy black ribbon. Back then, Americans got their news from newspapers and magazines, AM radio, and black-and-white television. By the time I retired in 2013, journalists were writing on sleek laptop computers and more and more people were getting their news from wireless phones whose capabilities were unimaginable in the days when rotary dials were state of the art.

As a young girl dreaming of working in journalism, I had no inkling I would spend virtually my whole career in television news. I made that decision as a senior at Brown University when President John F. Kennedy was assassinated. That was the moment I realized the immediacy of television news.

I first became aware of the idea of television when my dad, listening to the World Series on radio said, "Someday you'll be *seeing* the game on television." He was correct. And it wasn't long before television surpassed newspapers and radio as the number one source of news.

In my lifetime, I watched as television grew rapidly. Black-and-white screens turned to living color, film gave way to videotape—bringing much-needed speed to TV news—sound went from mono to stereo, cathode ray tubes were replaced by flat panels, and the signal changed from analog to digital.

There is no longer a regular news cycle ending at dinner time or 11:00 p.m. News is now on a twenty-four-hour cycle, instantly reported all day as it develops. Viewers seem content to watch or read the fragments from their phones and just want piecemeal content rather than an entire broadcast.

I witnessed many changes in my six decades in journalism. But the biggest changes for me personally came in 2013.

# 23

## OFF THE CLOCK
### Life after CBS News

So much of television news is about time. There are time deadlines to meet. Stories must be told and programs aired in a limited amount of time. The difference between getting a good story and missing it can be a matter of being in the right place at the right time. I was fortunate enough to be at CBS News at just the right time. The Golden Years. But by the middle of my fifth decade at CBS, the glitter at the Tiffany Network had long since faded and it was time for me to think about calling an end to my career.

When I joined CBS News in the 1960s, there were only three commercial television networks—ABC, CBS, and NBC. Hundreds of millions of Americans had just three choices for network news, and CBS was often their first choice. The network news divisions were run as a public service, paid for in part out of the huge profits from sports and entertainment programming.

That all began to change in the 1980s. New corporate owners demanded that news make a profit. Budgets were slashed. Jobs cut. And the networks felt growing competition for viewers, first from cable television and later digital platforms.

As the networks tried to hold viewers, news changed radically. Reporting, as I had practiced it, became much more personal and not as measured as I was used to. In 2011, I began to plan my exit, signing an agreement to retire in two years, at the end of February 2013.

I had a wonderful send-off, first in the CBS newsroom, surrounded by scores of colleagues, and several weeks later, a more personal dinner with close friends. Hundreds of people responded to news of my retirement with e-mails. Three of them stand out for me and always will:

Producer Dana Roberson wrote: "I am forever grateful to you, Linda, for giving me my first job . . . It was the beginning of a fulfilling career for me and you have always been a role model . . . You juggled parenthood and work in a way that made me believe that I could have a successful career and be a good mom, too."

Los Angeles Bureau Chief Eleanor Vega wrote: "Thank you for guiding and inspiring young journalists like me. We are better because of you."

Correspondent Armen Keteyian wrote: "You are truly one of a kind—an executive who not only walked in our shoes but created the path so many others have followed. I could always count on you to listen and offer careful, clear-eyed counsel. You knew. You cared. It showed."

And Bill Moyers, who had worked with me at the *CBS Evening News*, wrote, "You made a remarkable contribution to journalism over your many years at CBS. I don't know how you managed to balance all the egos and dynamics through change after change and keep your personal poise and professional focus, but you did."

When I look back at my career and those farewell notes, I realize that one of my most fulfilling experiences was sharing advice with my colleagues and helping them solve problems. I feel proud of my contributions and privileged to have worked at CBS News, experiencing firsthand many of the great events of the past fifty years. From LBJ and Vietnam to the Reagan-Gorbachev summits and the fall of communism in Eastern Europe to political campaigns and the horror of 9/11, in our own backyard, I was always a part of the news as it was happening.

I was fortunate that the decision to retire was my own. It doesn't always happen that way. Shortly after I retired, CBS News bought out the contract of a fellow senior vice president. This was tantamount to being fired but allowed the employee to be paid the remainder of their salary. Several years later, contracts for another vice president and an executive producer were not renewed after more than thirty years of service.

I left on a Thursday, slept the weekend, and by Monday CBS was in my rearview mirror. To be sure, I missed my colleagues, but I also knew I had made the right choice. I felt strongly about continuing to remain active in the International Women's Media Foundation (IWMF), an organization that helps women journalists around the world. IWMF sponsors courses on safety in war zones, helps women journalists who suffer from emergency illness or death threats, and funds journalists' special projects.

About six months after retiring, I was invited to provide expertise to two law firms that were representing defendants in separate libel cases. My role as an expert witness was to examine the claims the plaintiff had made about libel and other issues. It was interesting judging the veracity of the reports from the other side. I examined both cases, felt journalistic standards had been met, and suggested strategies the lawyers could use to defend each organization.

One of the great things about retirement is the control I gained of my time. My husband and I have been free to travel. Our first trip was to Australia to attend the Australian Tennis Open—my husband is a tennis fanatic. We toured Australia and then went on to New Zealand. This was a wonderful, but tough, trip. I'm glad we did it first because I'm not sure we could tolerate the twenty-three-hour flights today. Some advice: Keep in mind that bucket list and do the more difficult things first. We have gone through the Panama Canal and re-visited various southeast Asian and European countries in wonderful trips free of pressure.

I go to a gym, practice yoga, and am probably more fit than I've been in years. I read. In pre-pandemic days, I went to concerts and theatre and have begun to do so again. Reliving my life in writing this memoir, I realize I was so lucky to see the world and to work with both people of power as well as "just folks." Both taught me so much.

I could not have done it without my rock, my husband, Cary Aminoff. Together we could coordinate activities with our daughters, Beth and Elissa. Cary knew I needed to be out in the world and he supported me in my careers: CBS, wife, and mom.

Do I miss working? No. Now I have plenty of time for my grandson, family, and friends. I have time to read and travel and garden, to celebrate special occasions, and to sleep in when I choose. I have slowed down. I take time to smell the roses. So much of life is about time. And it's been a lovely time.

# ACKNOWLEDGMENTS

This memoir might have never come to be if I had not mentioned my intentions to a good friend who introduced me to Joelle Sander, formerly a professor and associate director at the Sarah Lawrence Center for Continuing Education. Sander taught memoir writing as well as courses in the essay and on modern poetry. She also wrote the prize-winning book *Before Their Time: Four Generations of Teenage Mothers*.

Sander looked at my draft and deemed it a news report with nothing about me. With patience she helped guide me to share my feelings and emotions chapter by chapter and was always encouraging.

A big thanks to Jerry Cipriano, who helped smooth and energize my prose. Jerry is the best writer and editor I have worked with, an opinion shared by many colleagues at CBS News. After beginning his career as a writer at AP (the Associated Press), he joined CBS News and worked as a writer and then news editor at the *CBS Evening News* for thirty-four years. He was used to writing the first draft of history. But he was so much more. He sprinkled his magic over my prose, smoothing it out and making it flow. He is a true friend, eager to help others. It may sound oxymoronic, but he is a news writer with a touch of the poet.

Natalie Mandziuk, my editor at Rowman & Littlefield, was a wonderful surprise. She was a pleasure to work with—encouraging me and making some very important comments to improve the memoir.

Hugs to my family, Cary, Beth, and Elissa, who were encouraging and loving during the whole journey. And a special thanks to Elissa, who helped me with the computer time and again as we prepared the manuscript.

# SOURCES

## CHAPTER 4

Brinkley, Douglas. *Cronkite*. New York. Harper Collins. 2012. pp.105–7.

## CHAPTER 7

US District Court of Central California, Judge Warren Ferguson. Morris Diamond versus CBS, Linda Mason and David Culhane, No. CV75 2638. Reporter's partial transcript of proceedings, May 11, 1978, pp. 1–4.
Findings of fact and conclusions of Law, June 2, 1978, pp. 6–7.

## CHAPTER 17

Election Night Coverage by the Networks before House Committee on Energy and Commerce, serial no. 107–25, February 14, 2001.
Report of the Independent Review Panel . . . Dick Thornburgh and Louis Boccardi. January 5, 2005. Examination of the September 8, 2004 (CBS News), *60 Minutes* Segment "For the Record."

## CHAPTER 19

Mapes, Mary. *Truth and Duty*. New York. St. Martin's Press. November 2005.

## CHAPTER 20

Dozier, Kimberly. *Breathing the Fire*. Des Moines, Iowa. Meredith Books. 2008.

## CHAPTER 22

*Full Circle*. Carl Bernstein talks with CNN's Anderson Cooper. January 4, 2022.

# INDEX

# ABOUT THE AUTHOR

**Linda S. Mason** is the former senior vice president for standards and special projects at CBS News and was responsible for two of CBS News' weekend broadcasts: *Sunday Morning* and the *CBS Evening News*. She was the CBS News representative for National Election Pool (NEP). Mason also oversaw *CBS Reports*, a documentary series for which she served as executive producer. Prior to her management assignments, Mason was executive producer of *CBS News Sunday Morning* (1987–1992) and of CBS News' three weekend broadcasts (1986–1992). Mason was a producer and then senior producer for the *CBS Evening News* (1971–1986) during the anchorships of both Walter Cronkite and Dan Rather. She became the first female producer on the broadcast when she joined it as a field producer in 1971. She was a writer/associate producer for the *CBS Morning News* (1968–1970). Before that, Mason was a news writer at WCBS-TV, the CBS-owned station in New York. She joined CBS News in January 1966 as a radio desk assistant. Over the years, Mason won thirteen Emmys, was awarded Brown University's prestigious William Roger's Award, and was inducted into the Deadline Club's Hall of Fame.

9 781538 176405